Mass. Ordinances Worcester

Laws and Ordinances of the City of Worcester

Mass. Ordinances Worcester

Laws and Ordinances of the City of Worcester

ISBN/EAN: 9783337232504

Printed in Europe, USA, Canada, Australia, Japan

Cover: Foto ©Suzi / pixelio.de

More available books at **www.hansebooks.com**

AND

ORDINANCES

OF THE

CITY OF WORCESTER.

1880.

WORCESTER:

PRESS OF SNOW, WOODMAN & COMPANY,

47 MAIN STREET.

PREFACE.

IN preparing, for publication, the laws and ordinances of the City of Worcester, the committee of the city council, having the matter in charge, have decided to present, in connection therewith, such, only, of the acts of the Legislature, as seemed to be of special and permanent interest. As a matter of historical interest, however, they have included the Act of June 14, 1722, incorporating the town of Worcester, and a list of all members of the city council since the incorporation of the city. The foregoing, together with the rules and orders of the city council, and of the two branches thereof, comprise most of the matter that it has been deemed advisable to include in the present compilation. In carrying out the details of this plan, it will be observed that much of the material included in the revision of 1867 has been omitted, but, as copies of that work are still readily accessible, it is not believed that any inconvenience will result therefrom.

In all matters pertaining to the powers and duties of municipal governments, reference must often be had to the Statutes of the Commonwealth, as well as to the decisions of the Supreme Judicial Court relative thereto. While not undertaking the preparation of a digest of these statutes, or of the numerous judicial decisions thereon, the committee have endeavored, by suitable references, to indicate wherein the city charter and other special laws have been modified by subsequent legislation.   To some extent, also, they have endeavored to show the authority under which the various ordinances of the city have been passed by the city council. Further than that, especially in view of the fact that a commission is now engaged in a revision of the general laws of the State, the committee have not considered it necessary or desirable to furnish additional notes and references for publication.

> FRANK H. KELLEY,
> HENRY A. MARSH,
> GEORGE F. HEWETT.
> OLIVER P. SHATTUCK,
> SAMUEL. A. PORTER,
> FRANCIS PLUNKETT,
> ALBERT. S. BROWN.

Contents.

TOWN OF WORCESTER.

IN THE REIGN OF KING GEORGE I.

An Act to incorporate the Town of Worcester,

Passed at a Great and General Court or Assembly for his Majesty's Provinces of the Massachusetts Bay in New England, begun and held at Boston, upon Wednesday the thirtieth day of May, 1722, being called by his Majesty's writs.

Resolved,—That the inhabitants of Worcester be vested with the powers and privileges of other towns within this Province; and that it be earnestly recommended to that Council only of the seven churches which did meet at Worcester in September 1721, to whom the contending parties submitted their differences relating to the Rev. Mr. Andrew Gardner, that the said council proceed and go to Worcester on or before the first Wednesday in September next, to finish what is further necessary to be done for the procuring and establishing of peace in the said town,

Inhabitants vested with the powers and privileges of towns.

Council of the seven churches recommended to go to Worcester to establish peace among the inhabitants.

Freeholders and inhabitants to assemble to choose town officers.

according to the submission of the parties ; and that the Freeholders and inhabitants of Worcester be assembled on the last Wednesday in September next, at ten o'clock in the forenoon, to choose all town officers as by law accustomed for towns to do at their annual meeting in March ; and that, at the opening of the meeting, they first proceed to the choice of a Moderator by written votes.

June 14th, 1722.   Consented to,

SAM'L SHUTE, Governor.

CITY CHARTER.

[STATUTE 1866, CHAPTER 199.]

AN ACT TO REVISE AND CONSOLIDATE THE CHARTER OF
THE CITY OF WORCESTER.

Be it enacted, &c., as follows:

SECT. 1.   The inhabitants of the City of Worcester Inhabitants to continue a body politic and corporate, shall continue to be a body politic and corporate, politic and corporate. under the name of the City of Worcester, and as such shall have, exercise and enjoy all the rights, immunities, powers and privileges, and shall be subject to all the duties and obligations now incumbent upon, and appertaining to, said city as a municipal corporation.

SECT. 2.   The administration of all the fiscal, Government: mayor, aldermen and common council. prudential and municipal affairs of said city, with the government thereof, shall be vested in one principal officer, to be styled the mayor; one council of eight, to be called the board of aldermen ; and one council of twenty-four, to be called the common council, which boards, in their joint capacity, shall be denominated the city council ; and the members thereof

Shall be sworn.

shall be sworn to the faithful performance of the duties of their respective offices.   A majority of each

Quorum.

board shall constitute a quorum for the transaction of business, and no member of either board shall receive any compensation for his services.[1]

Wards of city, council to establish in '75, and after decennially.

SECT. 3.   It shall be the duty of the city council, in the year eighteen hundred and seventy-five, and in every tenth year thereafter, and not oftener, to revise, and if it be needful, make a new division of the city into eight wards, so that they shall contain, as nearly as may be consistent with well defined limits to each ward, an equal number of voters in each ward according to the census to be taken in the month of

Existing wards to remain.

May in said years; and until such new division be made, the boundary lines of the wards shall remain as now established.

Annual election.

SECT. 4.   The election of city and ward officers shall take place on the second Monday of December[2]

Municipal year.

of each year, and the municipal year shall begin on the first Monday of January following.

Election of ward officers.

SECT. 5.   On the second Monday of December,[2] annually, there shall be chosen by ballot, in each o

---

1 For provisions concerning contracts with the city, see St. 1875, chap. 232.

2 By St. 1874, chap. 376, sec. 53, the municipal election is now held on the Tuesday next after said second Monday. For School Committee, see note 2, sec. 26.

said wards, a warden, clerk, and three inspectors of
elections,[1] residents of the wards in which they are
chosen, who shall hold their offices for the municipal
year next following, and until others shall have been
chosen in their places and qualified to act; and in
case of a failure to elect any one or more of said
officers at the annual meeting of any of said wards,
then said ward meetings may be adjourned from time Adjournment of
meetings in case
to time, until such election is completed.   It shall be of failure.
the duty of such warden to preside at all ward meetings, with the powers of moderator of town meetings.
And if, at any such meeting, the warden shall not
be present, the clerk of such ward shall call the
meeting to order, and preside until a warden *pro* Presiding officers
at ward meetings.
tempore shall be chosen by ballot.   And if, at any
meeting, the clerk shall not be present, a clerk *pro-*
tempore shall be chosen by ballot.   The clerk shall Clerk of ward,
duties.
record all the proceedings, and certify the votes
given, and deliver over to his successor in office all
such records and journals, together with all other
documents and papers held by him in said capacity.

---

1 By St. 1877, chap. 209, (accepted by the city October 15th, 1877,) the
mayor and aldermen shall, before the first day of November in each year,
elect for each ward of the city one inspector of elections, who shall be a
qualified voter and an inhabitant in such ward, and shall hold office for three
years from the first day of November then next succeeding, and may be
removed by a two-thirds vote of the board of aldermen.   They shall perform
such duties as are required of inspectors of elections under existing laws, but
the voters still elect inspectors.

Inspectors.

It shall be the duty of the inspectors of elections to assist the warden in receiving, assorting and counting the votes. And the warden, clerk and inspectors so chosen shall respectively make oath faithfully and impartially to discharge their several duties relative to all elections, which oath may be administered by the clerk of such ward to the warden, and by the warden to the clerk and inspectors, or by any justice of the peace for the county of Worcester. A certificate that the oath has been taken shall be entered upon the records of the ward by the clerk thereof.

Oaths of ward officers.

Certificates of oath.

Warrants for meetings.

SECT. 6. All warrants for the meetings of the citizens for municipal purposes, to be held either in wards or in general meetings, shall be issued by the mayor and aldermen, and shall be in such form,[1] and shall be served, executed and returned in such manner and at such time, as the city council may by any by-law direct.

Ward rooms, location of in certain contingency.

SECT. 7. The mayor and aldermen are authorized, when no convenient ward room for holding ward meetings of the citizens of either of the wards of the city can be had within the territorial limits of such

---

1 For warrants for election of representative to General Court see St. 1874, c. 376, sec. 24. For national, state, district and county officers, see Secs. 19–20, For all elections see St. 1878, c. 233.

ward, to appoint and direct, in the warrants for calling the ward meetings of such wards, the said meetings to be held in some convenient and proximate place within the limits of any other of the wards of said city ; and, for such purposes, the place so assigned for the meeting of such ward shall be deemed and taken to be included in and part of said ward, as though the same was within the territorial limits thereof.

SECT. 8.   The mayor shall be elected by the qualified voters of the city at large, voting in their respective wards, and shall hold his office for the municipal year next following his election, and until another shall be elected and qualified in his place. *Mayor, how chosen and tenure.*

[SECT. 9.   Eight aldermen, one alderman being selected from[1] each ward, shall be elected by the qualified voters of the city at large, voting in their respective wards, who shall hold their offices for one year from the first Monday of January next following their election, and until a majority of the new board shall be elected and qualified in their places. *Aldermen, number, how chosen and tenure.*

SECT. 10.   Three common councilmen shall be elected from[1] and by the voters of each ward, who shall, at the time of their election, be residents of the wards respectively in which they are elected, and shall hold their offices for one year from the first Monday of January next following their election.] *Councilmen, election, residence and tenure.*

---

1 Superseded by secs. 38 and 39.   See sec. 42.

Annual election:
Mayor,aldermen,
and councilmen. SECT. 11. On the second Monday of December[1] annually, the qualified voters in the several wards shall give in their votes by ballot for mayor, aldermen and common councilmen, in accordance with the provisions of this act; and all the votes so given shall be assorted, counted, declared and recorded in open ward meeting by causing the names of persons voted for, and the number of votes given for each, to be written in the ward record at length. The

Certificates of
election, duties of
ward clerks. clerk of the ward, within twenty-four hours after such election, shall deliver to the persons elected members of the common council, certificates of their elections, respectively, signed by the warden and clerk, and by a majority of the inspectors of elections, and shall deliver to the city clerk a copy of the record of such elections, certified in like manner;

Proviso. *provided*, *however*, that if the choice of members of the common council shall not be effected on that day, in any ward, the meeting in such ward may be adjourned, from time to time, to complete such election. The board of aldermen shall, as soon as

Mayor elect to be
notified. conveniently may be,[2] examine the copies of the records of the several wards, certified as aforesaid, and shall cause the person who shall have been

---

[1] On the Tuesday after the second Monday. See note 2 in sec. 4.

[2] By St. 1876, chap. 188, the board of aldermen shall not declare the result of an election less than three, nor more than five days (Sundays excepted) next following the date thereof.

elected mayor to be notified, in writing, of his election; but if it shall appear that no person has received a majority of the votes, or if the person elected shall refuse to accept the office, the board shall issue warrants for a new election, and the same proceedings shall be had, in all respects, as are herein before provided for the choice of mayor, and, from time to time, shall be repeated, until a mayor shall be chosen, and shall accept said office. In case of the decease,[1] resignation or absence of the mayor, or of his inability to perform the duties of his office, it shall be the duty of the board of aldermen and the common council, respectively, by vote, to declare that a vacancy exists, and the cause thereof; and, thereupon, the two boards shall meet in convention, and elect a mayor to fill such vacancy; and the mayor thus elected shall hold his office until the inability causing such vacancy shall be removed, or until a new election. If it shall appear that the whole number of aldermen have not been elected, the same proceedings shall be had as are herein before provided in regard to the choice of mayor. Each alderman shall be notified in writing of his election, by the mayor and aldermen for the time being.

Proceedings in case of failure to elect.

Mayor, vacancy in office, how filled.

Aldermen, vacancies, how filled.

Notice of election.

---

1 By St. 1871, chap. 1, printed herein, whenever the mayor elect shall die before entering upon the discharge of his duties, it is the duty of the board of aldermen and of the common council, respectively, by vote, to declare that fact; and the board of aldermen issue their warrant for an election to fill the vacancy.

Oath of mayor.   The oath prescribed by this act shall be administered to the mayor by the city clerk, or by any
justice of the peace for the county of Worcester.

Aldermen and   The aldermen and common councilmen elect shall,
council, oaths of. on the first Monday of January, at ten o'clock in the
forenoon, meet in convention, when the oath required
by this act shall be administered to the members of
the two boards present, by the mayor, or any justice
of the peace for the county of Worcester; and a
certificate of such oath having been taken shall be
entered on the journal of the mayor and aldermen,
and of the common council, by their respective clerks.

Record, in case   And whenever it shall appear that a mayor has not
mayor is not   been elected previously to the first Monday of Janu-
elected.   ary aforesaid, the mayor and aldermen, for the time
being, shall make a record of that fact, an attested
copy of which the city clerk shall read at the
opening of the convention, to be holden as aforesaid.

Organization of   After the oath has been administered as aforesaid,
council.   the two boards shall separate, and the common
council shall be organized by the choice of a president and clerk, to hold their offices, respectively,
during the pleasure of the common council; the
clerk to be under oath faithfully to perform the duties
of his said office.

Organization in   In case of the absence of the mayor elect on the
absence of   first Monday of January, or if a mayor shall not
mayor.   then have been elected, the city council shall organ-

ize itself in the manner herein before provided, and
may proceed to business in the same manner as if the
mayor were present; and the oath of office may, at
any time thereafter, in convention of the two boards,
be administered to the mayor, and any member of
the city council who may have been absent at the
organization.

In the absence of the mayor the board of aldermen Chairman of
aldermen pro
may choose a presiding officer, *pro tempore*, who shall tempore.
also preside at joint meetings of the two boards. Records of
boards.
Each board shall keep a record of its own proceedings,
and judge of the elections of its own members; and
in case of failure of election, or in case of vacancy, Vacancies.
declared by either board, the mayor and aldermen
shall issue their warrants for a new election.

SECT. 12. The mayor shall be the chief executive Mayor, powers
and duties
officer of the city. It shall be his duty to be vigilant defined.
and active in causing the laws and regulations of the
city to be enforced, and to keep a general supervision
over the conduct of all subordinate officers. And he
may, whenever in his opinion the public good may
require, remove, with the consent of the appointing
power, any officer over whose appointment he has,
in accordance with the provisions of this charter,
exercised the power of nomination.

He may call special meetings of the boards of
aldermen and common council, or either of them,

when, in his opinion, the interests of the city require it, by causing notices to be left at the usual place of residence of each member of the board or boards to be convened.

He shall, from time to time, communicate to both boards such information, and recommend such measures, as the business and interests of the city may, in his opinion, require.

He shall preside in the board of aldermen, and in convention of the two boards, but shall have a casting vote only.[1]

Salary.

The salary of the mayor shall be fixed by the city council, and made payable at stated periods, but shall not at any time exceed fifteen hundred dollars, nor shall it be increased or diminished during the year for which he is chosen.

General executive power vested in mayor and aldermen.

SECT. 13. The executive power of said city generally, and the administration of the police, with all the powers heretofore vested in the selectmen of Worcester, shall be vested in, and may be exercised by the mayor and aldermen, as fully as if the same were herein specially enumerated.

Appointments. police.

The mayor and aldermen shall have full and exclusive power to appoint a constable or constables, and a city marshal and assistants, with the powers

---

1 By St. 1876, chap. 193, he has no vote in the board of aldermen, but he has a veto power.

and duties of constables and all other police officers, and the same to remove at pleasure.[1] And the mayor and aldermen may require any person, who may be appointed marshal or constable of the city, to give bonds for the faithful discharge of the duties of the office, with such security, and to such amount, as they may deem reasonable and proper, upon which bonds the like proceedings and remedies may be had, *May require bonds.* as are by law provided in case of constables' bonds taken by the selectmen of towns.

The mayor and aldermen[2] shall have the care and *Shall have custody of public property.* superintendence of the city buildings and the custody and management of all city property, with power to let or to sell what may be legally sold, and to purchase property, real or personal, in the name and for the use of the city, whenever its interest or convenience may, in their judgment, require it. And *Shall publish receipts, and expenditures, with property and debts.* the mayor and aldermen shall, as often as once a year, cause to be published, for the use of the inhabitants, a particular account of the receipts and expenditures, and a schedule of city property and of the city debts.

---

1 By St. 1867, chap. 279, they "may at any time appoint police officers with all or any of the powers of constable, except the power of serving and executing civil processes, who shall fill their offices during the pleasure of the mayor and aldermen."

2 By St. 1873, chap. 183, printed herein, control of city property including school houses, is vested in the city council.

Shall have juris-   The mayor and aldermen shall have power to fix
diction over Mill
Brook.   the boundaries of Mill Brook, in said city, between
                     the factory buildings formerly of Rice, Fox and
                     Company and Grove Mills, and to alter, change,
                     widen, straighten and deepen the channel thereof,
                     and remove obstructions therefrom, as the public
                     good may require. And any damages sustained by
Damages, how   any person in his property by reason thereof, shall be
assessed.
                     assessed in the same manner, and upon the same
                     principles, as damages are assessed in the laying out
                     of town ways.

Mayor to have   SECT. 14.   In all cases in which appointments are
office nominating
power.   directed to be made by the mayor and aldermen, the
                     mayor shall have the exclusive power of nomination,
                     being subject, however, to confirmation or rejection
Incompatible   by the board of aldermen;[1] and no person shall be
offices.
                     eligible by appointment or election to any office of
                     emolument, the salary of which is payable out of
                     the city treasury, who, at the time of such appoint-
                     ment or election, shall be a member of the board of
Sittings of city   aldermen or of the common council. All sittings of
council, except
executive, to be   the mayor and aldermen, of the common council and
public.   of the city council, shall be public, when they are not
                     engaged in executive business.

_____

      1 St. 1876, chap. 80, provides that "if a person so nominated shall be
rejected, it shall be the duty of the mayor to make another nomination within
a month from the time of such rejection."

SECT. 15. The city council shall annually, as soon after their organization as may be convenient, elect, by joint ballot in convention, a treasurer and collector of taxes, city clerk, water commissioner, commissioner of highways, city solicitor, city auditor and city physician,[1] who shall hold their offices respectively for the term of one year, and until their successors shall be chosen and qualified : *provided, however,* that either of the officers named in this section may be removed at any time by the city council, for sufficient cause.

Treasurer, city clerk, water commissioner, commissioner of highways, solicitor, auditor and city physician, council to elect.

Removal.

SECT. 16. . The city council shall, in the month of December, annually, elect by joint ballot, in convention, a chief engineer of the fire department,[2] and as many assistant engineers, not exceeding six, as they may deem expedient, who shall hold their offices for the term of one year from the first Monday of January next ensuing, and until their successors are chosen and qualified.[3]

Chief engineer of fire department and assistants.

The compensation of all officers named in this and

Compensation of officers.

---

1 By St. 1877, chap. 133, (accepted by the legal voters, November 6, 1877,) the city physician is a member of the board of health, and by St. 1878, chap. 21, "where the city physician is *ex officio* a member of the board of health said city physician shall be appointed by the mayor, with the approval of the board of aldermen, for a term of three years; and shall be subject to removal, for cause, by the same authority."

2 For fire department, see St. 1868, chap. 195, printed herein.

3 See ordinances, chap. 7, for election of other officers.

the preceding section shall be fixed by concurrent vote of the city council.

SECT. 17. The city clerk shall also be clerk of the board of aldermen, and shall be sworn to the faithful performance of his duties. He shall perform such duties as shall be prescribed by the board of aldermen ; and he shall perform all the duties, and exercise all the powers by law incumbent upon him.

He shall deliver to his successor in office, as soon as chosen and qualified, all journals, records, papers, documents or other things held by him in his capacity of city clerk.

SECT. 18. The city council shall, in such manner as they shall determine, appoint or elect all other subordinate officers, for whose election or appointment other provision is not herein made, define their duties and fix their compensations.

SECT. 19. The city council shall take care that no money be paid from the treasury, unless granted or appropriated, and shall secure a just and proper accountability by requiring bonds, with sufficient penalties and sureties, from all persons interested with the receipt, custody or disbursement of money.

SECT. 20. The city council shall have power to lay out sidewalks,[1] and fix the width, height and grade of

---

1 See act concerning sidewalks, printed herein.

the same, and require all persons owning land abutting on such sidewalks to pave the walks with brick, stone, or concrete, and to keep the same in good repair, as they may direct, the city first setting the curbstones and paving the gutters; and in case any person, owning land as aforesaid, shall neglect or refuse to comply with the requirements of the city council after receiving due notice of such requirements, the city council shall have power to cause said sidewalks to be paved and kept in good repair, according to said requirement, and may recover of said owner, by an action on the case in the name of the city, the expense of paving and keeping the same in good repair.   The city council shall also have power to establish fire limits within the city, and from time to time change or enlarge the same; and by ordinance they shall regulate the construction of all buildings erected within said fire limits, stipulating their location, sizes and the material of which they shall be constructed, together with such other rules and regulations as shall tend to insure the same from damage by fire

Establishment of fire districts.

Regulations in construction of buildings.

SECT. 21. The city council is authorized to elect, by joint ballot in convention, a board of three commissioners, one member thereof to be elected each and every year, in the month of January, to hold office for the term of three years, who shall have the sole

Board of commissioners of public grounds, council may elect.

2

care, superintendence and management of the public
grounds belonging to said city of Worcester, and of
all the shade and ornamental trees standing and
growing thereon, and also of all the shade and
ornamental trees standing and growing in or upon
any of the public streets and highways of said city:
but said board, or any member thereof, after having
had an opportunity to be heard in his or their defence,
may be removed at any time, by a concurrent vote
of two-thirds of each branch of the city council; and
in case of a vacancy in said board of commissioners
by death, resignation, removal or otherwise, such
vacancy shall be filled by the choice of another
commissioner in the manner aforesaid, who shall hold
his office for the remainder of the term for which the
member in whose place he shall be elected would
have held the same.   Said board may be organized
by the choice of a chairman and secretary from their
own number, and a major part of said board shall
constitute a quorum for the transaction of business.

The said board of commissioners shall lay out said
public grounds,[1] or such part thereof as they shall
from time to time judge proper; and it shall be the
duty of said commissioners, from time to time, as
appropriations shall be made therefor by the city
council, to cause all necessary paths and avenues to

Vacancies and removal in board.

Organization.

Duties.

---

1 Laying out streets, &c., in.   See St. 1875, chap. 163.

be constructed therein, and to cause said public
grounds to be planted and embellished with trees, as
they shall think proper; and said commissioners shall
also cause such shade and ornamental trees to be
planted in and upon said public streets and highways
in said city as they shall think proper, and as appropriations shall be made therefor by the city council,
and shall adopt and use all necessary and proper
means to preserve the same, and promote the growth
thereof. And said board may make all necessary _{May make by-}
by-laws and regulations in the execution of their _{laws.}
trust, not inconsistent with this act and the laws of
the Commonwealth, as they shall deem expedient.

Said board of commissioners shall, annually, in the _{Shall make}
month of January, and whenever required by the _{report of their doings.}
city council, make and render a report of all their
acts and doings, and of the condition of the public
grounds and shade and ornamental trees thereon, and
on said streets and highways, and an account of
receipts and expenditures for the same.

SECT. 22. The city council is authorized to elect, _{Board of commissioners}
by joint ballot in convention, a board of five com- _{of Hope Ceme-}
_{tery, council may}
missioners, one member thereof to be elected each _{elect.}
and every year, in the month of January, to hold
office for the term of five years, who shall have the
sole care, superintendence and management of " Hope
Cemetery," established by said city council; but said

board, or any member thereof, after having had an opportunity to be heard in his or their defence, may be removed at any time by a concurrent vote of two-thirds of each branch of the city council; and in case of a vacancy in said board of commissioners, by death, resignation, removal or otherwise, such vacancy shall be filled by the choice of another commissioner, in the manner aforesaid, who shall hold his office for the remainder of the term for which the member in whose place he shall be elected would have held the same. Said board may be organized by the choice of a chairman and secretary from their own number, and a major part of said board shall constitute a quorum for the transaction of business.

The said board of commissioners shall lay out said cemetery, or such part thereof as is not already laid out, into such lots or subdivisions for burial places as they shall think proper, and the said commissioners shall set apart a proper portion of said cemetery for a public burial place for the use of the inhabitants of said city free of charge thereof; and it shall be the duty of said commissioners, from time to time, as appropriations shall be made by the city council therefor, to cause all necessary paths and avenues to be constructed therein, and to cause said cemetery to be planted and embellished with trees, shrubs, flowers and other rural ornaments, as they shall think proper; and said board may make all necessary by-laws and

Vacancies and removals in board.

Organization.

Duties and powers.

regulations in the execution of their trust, not inconsistent with this act and the laws of the Commonwealth, as they shall deem expedient.

Said board of commissioners shall have authority
to sell to any person or persons the sole and exclusive ^May sell right in cemetery, &c.^
right of burial,[1] and of erecting tombs, cenotaphs and
other monuments, in any of the designated lots or
subdivisions of said cemetery, upon such terms and
conditions as they shall, by their rules and regulations,
prescribe ; but all deeds and conveyances of such lots
or rights of burial shall be made in the name of the ^Deeds and conveyances,^
city, and shall be executed in behalf of the city by ^how made.^
the treasurer thereof, for the time being, when requested so to do by said commissioners ; and the
proceeds of such sales shall in all cases be paid into
the city treasury. Said board of commissioners shall
annually, in the month of January, and whenever
required by the city council, make and render a ^Shall make^
report of all their acts, doings and proceedings, and ^report of their doings.^
of the condition of the cemetery, and an account of
the receipts and expenditures for the same.

SECT. 23. The board of overseers of the poor in ^Board of over-^
the city of Worcester shall consist of nine members, ^seers of poor.^
residents of said city. The mayor, superintendent of

---

1 The title is indivisible ; see St. 1877, chap. 182, § 4, by which Gen'l St.
chap. 28, § 3. applies.

Ex-officio members.
public schools and the city marshal shall be *ex-officio* members of the board. The mayor shall be *ex-officio* president of the board. The city council shall elect

Election and tenure of office.
by joint ballot six persons to be members of said board of overseers, two to be elected in the month of December in each year, and to hold their offices for the term of three years from the third Monday of January then next ensuing, and until others shall be elected and qualified in their places. But no more than one of the six members, so to be elected, shall be eligible from any one ward of said city.

Vacancies, how filled.
Vacancies occurring in the board may be filled by joint ballot of the city council, at any time, the member so elected to hold office for only the unexpired term of the member who has ceased to hold

Removals.
office. The city council shall also have power, at any time, for cause, to remove either of said over-

Organization of board.
seers from office. The board shall be organized, annually, on the third Monday of January.

Duties.
Said overseers shall perform the duties of the overseers of the poor, of the directors of the almshouse, and of the truant commissioners in the city of Worcester, as required by the statutes of the Commonwealth, and subject to the ordinances of the city of Worcester, and there shall be elected no other officers for the performance of said duties in said city.

Assessors.
SECT. 24. The city council shall elect by joint

ballot, in convention, three persons to be assessors of taxes, one person to be elected in the month of February or March in each year, whose compensation shall be fixed by concurrent vote of the city council, and to hold office for the term of three years from his election. The persons so chosen shall constitute the board of assessors, and shall exercise the powers and be subject to the duties and liabilities of assessors in towns. Compensation and tenure. Powers and duties.

In case of a vacancy in said board of assessors, by death, resignation, removal or otherwise, such vacancy shall be filled by the choice of another assessor in the manner aforesaid, who shall hold his office for the unexpired term for which the member in whose place he shall be elected would have held the same. All taxes shall be assessed, apportioned and collected in the manner prescribed by the general laws of the Commonwealth : *provided, however,* that the city council may establish further or additional provisions for the collection thereof. Vacancies, how filled. Taxes, how assessed, &c. Proviso.

SECT. 25. The qualified voters of each ward, at their respective annual ward meetings for the choice of officers, shall elect, by ballot, one person in each ward, who shall be a resident of said ward, to be an assistant-assessor ; and it shall be the duty of the persons so chosen to furnish the assessors with all necessary information relative to persons and property Assistant-assessors, election. Duties.

taxable in their respective wards; and they shall
be sworn to the faithful performance of their duty.

School commit-
tee, election.

SECT. 26. The qualified voters of each ward[1] shall
elect, by ballot, three persons in each ward, who
shall be residents of the ward, to be members of the

Tenure of office.

school committee,[2] one person to be chosen in each
ward at their respective annual meetings for the term
of three years; and the persons so chosen shall, with
the mayor, constitute the school committee, and have
the care and superintendence of the public schools.[3]

Support of
schools, rights
and obligations
heretofore con-
ferred to be
vested in city.

And all the rights and obligations of the town of
Worcester in relation to the grant and appropriation
of money to the support of schools, and the special
powers and authority heretofore conferred, by law,
upon the inhabitants of the centre school district in
said town, to raise money for the support of schools
in said district, shall be merged in the powers and
obligations of the city, to be exercised in the same
manner as over other subjects of taxation; and all

Appropriations
for, how made.

grants and appropriations of money for the support

1 By St. 1879, chap. 223, women may vote, and the election may, in the
discretion of the mayor and aldermen, be called on another day of the same
month as the city election.

2 By St. 1874, chap. 389, "no person shall be deemed ineligible to serve
on a school committee by reason of sex."

3 By St. 1874, chap. 272, the committee "may appoint and fix the compensation of a superintendent of public schools, a majority vote of the whole
board being necessary for that purpose."

of schools, and the erection and repair of school-houses, in said city, shall be made by the city council, in the same manner as grants and appropriations are made for other city purposes.

SECT. 27. Should there fail to be a choice of members of the school committee, or assistant-assessors in any ward, on the day of the annual ward meeting, the meeting shall be adjourned from time to time, until the elections shall be completed. *School committee and assistant assessors, election.*

SECT. 28. The city council shall have the same powers in relation to the laying out, acceptance, altering or discontinuing of streets and ways, and the assessment of damages, which selectmen and inhabitants of towns now have by law;[1] but all petitions and questions relating to laying out, widening, altering or discontinuing any street or way, shall be first acted on by the mayor and aldermen. *Laying out of streets, powers of city council.*

Any person aggrieved by any proceedings of the mayor and aldermen, or of the city council, in the exercise of such powers respecting streets and ways, shall have the same right of appeal, by complaint, to the county commissioners of the county of Worcester, *Appeals to county commissioners.*

---

1 If under the betterment law the decree should declare "the same to be laid out under the provision of law authorizing the assessment of betterments,"—St. 1874. chap. 275. For the betterment law, see St. 1871, chap. 382. In public commons, &c., see St. 1875, chap. 163.

as is given by the laws of the Commonwealth to appeal from the decisions of selectmen or the inhabitants of towns.[1]

Streets over private land, width prescribed.

SECT. 29.   No street or way shall hereafter be opened in the city of Worcester, over any private land, by the owners thereof, and dedicated to or permitted to be used by the public, of a less width than forty feet, except with the consent of said mayor and aldermen, in writing, first had and obtained for that purpose.[2]

Drains and sewers.

SECT. 30.   The city council shall have authority to cause drains and common sewers[3] to be laid down through any streets or private lands, paying the owners such damage as they may sustain thereby, said damage to be assessed in the same manner and upon the same principles as damages are assessed in the laying out of town ways, and to require all persons to pay a reasonable sum for the privilege of opening any drain into said public drain or common sewer; and also to require that private drains shall be conducted into the public drain or sewer, in any case in which the said city council shall judge the same necessary or proper for the 'cleanliness and health of the city.

1 St. 1873, chap. 261, provides for petition to the superior court.
2 See St. 1850, chap. 188, printed herein.
3 See acts concerning sewers and drains, printed herein.

SECT. 31.   The city council may make by-laws, Inspection of
with suitable penalties, for the inspection and survey, lumber, wood, hay, coal and
measurement and sale of lumber, wood, hay, coal and bark.
bark, brought into the city for sale, and shall have
the same powers as the town had in reference to the
fire department, and the laws relating thereto, and in
reference to the suspension of the laws for the protection and preservation of useful birds, and of all
other laws the operation or suspension of which is
subject to the action of the town thereon.

SECT. 32.   All elections of national, state, county Elections of
and district officers who are voted for by the people, national, state, county and
shall be held at meetings of the citizens qualified to district officers.
vote at such elections, in their respective wards, at
the time fixed by law for these elections respectively.

SECT. 33.   Prior to every election, the mayor and Lists of voters, how prepared.
aldermen¹ shall make out lists of all the citizens of
each ward qualified to vote in such elections, in the
manner in which selectmen of towns are required to
make out lists of voters; and, for that purpose, they
shall have full access to the assessors' books and lists,
and are empowered to call for the assistance of the
assessors, assistant-assessors, and other city officers ;
and they shall deliver the lists so prepared and

---

1 By St. 1877, chap. 193, printed herein, the duties of the mayor and aldermen about voting lists are devolved upon the registrars of voters. For other
provision as to elections, see St. 1874, chap. 376, and acts in amendment
thereof.

corrected to the clerks of the several wards, to be used at such elections; and no person shall be entitled to

vote whose name is not borne on such list. A list of the voters of each ward shall be posted in one or more public places in each ward: *provided, however*,[1]

that any person whose name shall not be borne on the list of the ward in which he is entitled to vote, when it shall be placed in the hands of the clerk of said ward, shall have the right to have his name entered thereon at any time thereafter before the closing of the polls, upon presenting to the ward officers a certificate, signed by the mayor or city clerk, setting forth his right to have his name so entered.

SECT. 34. General meetings of the citizens qualified to vote, may from time to time be held, to consult upon the public good, to instruct their representatives and to take all lawful means to obtain redress for any grievances, according to the right secured to the people by the constitution of this Commonwealth.

And such meetings may and shall be duly warned by the mayor and aldermen, upon the request in writing, setting forth the purposes thereof, of fifty qualified voters.

---

1 Names to be added only when qualifications are determined previous to the close of registration. St. 1874, chap. 376, sec. 10, as amended by St. 1877, chap. 193, sec. 5, printed herein.

Sect. 35. The city council shall have power to make all such salutary and needful by-laws as towns, by the laws of this Commonwealth, have power to make and establish, and to annex penalties, not exceeding twenty dollars, for the breach thereof, which by-laws shall take effect and be in force from and after the time therein respectively limited, without the sanction of any court or other authority whatever: *provided, however*, that all laws and regulations in force in the town of Worcester shall, until they shall expire by their own limitation, or be revised or repealed by the city council, remain in force; and all fines and forfeitures, for the breach of any by-law or ordinance, shall be paid into the city treasury.

Council may make by-laws and annex penalties.

Proviso.

Sect. 36. All the authority, powers, privileges, rights and obligations, created and given by section twenty-three, chapter thirty-two of the acts passed in the year one thousand eight hundred and forty-eight, entitled "An Act to establish the City of Worcester," and the "Act for supplying the City of Worcester with pure water," approved on the eighteenth of March, in the year one thousand eight hundred and sixty-four, shall be vested in and exercised by the city of Worcester, in such manner, by such officers, servants and agents as the city council shall from time to time ordain, appoint and direct.

Powers and obligations of Acts of '48 and '64 vested in city, under direction of council.

Sect. 37. Nothing in this act contained shall be

Legislature
may amend
Act.

so construed as to restrain or prevent the legislature
from amending or altering the same, whenever they
shall deem it expedient.

First election
of aldermen.

SECT. 38.   On the second Monday in December
in the year one thousand eight hundred and sixty-six
the qualified voters of the city, voting at large in
their respective wards, shall give in their votes for
eight aldermen, one alderman being selected from
each ward, whose term of office shall be as follows,

Tenures.

viz.: the aldermen thus elected for wards numbered
one, three, five and seven, shall hold their offices
respectively for the term of two municipal years next
following their election; and the aldermen thus
elected for the wards numbered two, four, six and
eight, shall hold their offices respectively for the term
of one municipal year next following their election;
and all elections of aldermen after said second Monday of December shall be for the term of two years
from the first Monday of January next following
their election; except elections to fill vacancies, in
which case the elections shall be for the unexpired
term only.

Election of
councilmen.

SECT. 39.   On the second Monday of December in
the year one thousand eight hundred and sixty-six
the qualified voters in each ward of the city shall
elect three common councilmen, who shall, at the

time of their election, be residents of the wards, respectively, in which they are elected, whose terms of office shall be as follows, viz.: at said election, Tenures. wards numbered two, four, six and eight shall elect two common councilmen each for the term of two municipal years, and one common councilman each for the term of one municipal year next following their election; wards numbered one, three, five and seven, shall at the same time elect one common councilman each for the term of two municipal years, and two common councilmen each for the term of one municipal year next following their election; and all elections of common councilmen after said second Monday of December shall be for the term of two years from the first Monday of January next following their election; except elections to fill vacancies, in which case the election shall be for the unexpired term only.

SECT. 40. All acts and parts of acts inconsistent Repeal. with this act are hereby repealed: *provided, however,* Provisos. that the repeal of the said acts shall not affect any act done, or any right accruing or accrued or established, or any suit or proceeding had or commenced in any civil case before the time when such repeal shall take effect; and that no offence committed, and no penalty or forfeiture incurred under the acts hereby repealed, and before the time when such repeal

shall take effect, shall be affected by the repeal; and
that no suit or prosecution pending at the time of
the said repeal for any offence committed, or for the
recovery of any penalty or forfeiture incurred under
the acts hereby repealed, shall be affected by such
repeal; and *provided, also*, that all persons who, at
the time when the said repeal shall take effect, shall
hold any office under the said acts, shall continue to
hold the same according to the tenure thereof; and
provided, also, that all the by-laws and ordinances of
the city of Worcester which shall be in force at the
time when the said repeal shall take effect, shall
continue in force until the same are repealed by the
city council, and all officers elected under such by-
laws and ordinances shall continue in office according to the tenure thereof.

Repeal not to
annul former
repeal.

SECT. 41. No act which has been heretofore
repealed shall be revived by the repeal of the acts
mentioned in the preceding section.

Is to be adopted
by inhabitants;
otherwise void.

SECT. 42. This act shall be void unless the inhabitants of the city of Worcester, at a legal meeting
called for that purpose, by a written vote determine
to adopt the same as hereinafter provided; all the
sections of this act except the thirty-eighth and
thirty-ninth, shall be voted for or against upon one
ballot; sections thirty-eight and thirty-nine shall be

voted for or against upon one ballot; and if sections Manner of meeting prescribed. thirty-eight and thirty-nine shall be accepted upon such vote, then sections nine and ten of this act shall be void, and sections thirty-eight and thirty-nine shall stand in place of sections nine and ten: *provided*, the other parts of this act shall be adopted by said inhabitants. The qualified voters of the city shall be called upon to give in their votes as aforesaid upon Proviso. the acceptance of this act in the manner aforesaid, at meetings in the various wards duly warned by the mayor and aldermen, to be held on or before the Tuesday next after the first Monday of November Meeting to be held on or before Tuesday after first Monday in November. next, and thereupon the same proceedings shall be had respecting the sorting, counting, declaring, recording and returns of said votes as is herein provided at the election of mayor and aldermen; and the board of mayor and aldermen shall, within three days thereafter, meet together and compare the returns of the ward officers, and if it shall appear that the inhabitants have voted to adopt this act as aforesaid, the mayor shall make proclamation Citizens adopting, mayor to proclaim and Act deemed in force. of the fact, and thereupon this act, or so much of it as shall have been adopted, shall take effect from and after the day on which the mayor shall make proclamation as aforesaid.

APPROVED APRIL 30, 1866.

The Charter, including sections thirty-eight and thirty-nine, was adopted June 11, 1866.

3

STATUTES.

STATUTE 1871.   CHAPTER 1.

AN ACT CONCERNING THE ELECTION OF MAYOR IN THE CITY OF WORCESTER.

Be it enacted, &c., as follows:

Aldermen may issue warrant for election of mayor. SECTION 1. The board of aldermen of the city of Worcester are hereby authorized to issue their warrant for the election of a mayor in place of James B. Blake, elected mayor at the last annual election held in said city, and since deceased; and the mayor elected in pursuance of such warrant, having first been duly qualified, shall hold his office until the termination of the present municipal year of said city, and until another shall be chosen and qualified in his place.

If mayor dies before entering upon duties, aldermen may issue warrant for new election. SECT. 2. Whenever the mayor elect of said city shall die before entering upon the discharge of his duties, it shall be the duty of the board of aldermen and of the common council of said city, respectively, by vote to declare that fact; and the board of aldermen shall thereupon issue their warrant for a new election of mayor, to be held at such 'time as they shall deem advisable ; and the mayor chosen at such election shall hold his office for the term for which such deceased mayor was elected, and until another is chosen and qualified in his place.

SECT. 3.   This act shall take effect upon its passage.

APPROVED JANUARY 14, 1871.

STATUTE 1873.   CHAPTER 183.

AN ACT TO AMEND THE CHARTER OF THE CITY OF WOR-
CESTER, RELATIVE TO THE PURCHASE AND CONTROL
OF CITY PROPERTY.

Be it enacted, &c., as follows :

SECTION 1.   The city council of the city of Wor- City council to have custody cester shall have the care and superintendence of and manage- ment of all city the school houses and other public buildings of said property. city, and the care, custody and management of all the property of said city, with power to lease or sell what may be legally sold.

And the said city council may purchase property, real or personal, in the name and for the use of said city, whenever its interest or convenience may in their judgment require it.

SECT. 2. So much of the thirteenth section of chapter one hundred and ninety-nine of the acts of the year eighteen hundred and sixty-six, as confers upon the mayor and aldermen of said city the powers herein granted to said city council, is repealed.

Repeal of part of statute of 1866, chap. 199, § 13.

SECT. 3. This act shall take effect upon its passage.

APPROVED APRIL 14, 1873.

STATUTE 1877. CHAPTER 193.

AN ACT TO ESTABLISH THE BOARD OF REGISTRARS OF VOTERS OF THE CITY OF WORCESTER, AND TO REGULATE THE PREPARATION AND REVISION OF THE VOTING LISTS IN SAID CITY.

Be it enacted, &c., as follows :

Registrars of voters to be elected.

SECT. 1. There shall be elected by the city council of the city of Worcester, as soon as may be after the passage of this act, and biennially thereafter in the month of February or March, one able and discreet person, an inhabitant of said city, who shall hold no other office or position by election or appointment under the government thereof, and who shall hold his office for two years and until another shall be elected in his place, who, together with the city clerk and the clerk of the board of assessors of said city,

shall constitute a board of registrars of voters. The
person elected as above shall serve as clerk of the
board, and in case of a vacancy by reason of death,
resignation or removal, the city council shall elect a
person qualified as aforesaid, to hold the office for
the residue of the term.

SECT. 2. The registrars shall, in addition to the To prepare and
duties imposed upon them by this act, perform all revise voting lists.
and singular, the duties devolved upon the mayor
and aldermen or board of aldermen by any general
or special laws which now are or hereafter may be in
force respecting the preparation, correction, revision,
publication and transmission to the ward officers, of
the alphabetical lists of voters to be used at elections
in said city, and all the powers so conferred, and all
the duties and liabilities so imposed upon the mayor
and aldermen or board of aldermen of said city in
relation to the preparation, correction, revision,
publication and transmission of said lists, are hereby
conferred and imposed exclusively upon said registrars.

SECT. 3. The registrars shall, before entering To be sworn.
upon the duties of their office, take and subscribe an
oath faithfully to perform the same. They shall
receive such compensation as the city council may Compensation.
from time to time determine, but such compensation
shall not be regulated by the number of names

registered on any list of voters, and any reduction of compensation shall take effect upon such registrars only as shall be elected after such reduction.

To prepare list of voters.

SECT. 4. The registrars shall prepare, correct, revise and publish, in accordance with this act and with the laws of the Commonwealth, the alphabetical lists of voters of each ward, and the collectors of taxes of said city shall make the return now required by law to be made to the mayor and aldermen, to the board of registrars of voters, and all assessors and collectors of taxes of said city shall furnish any information in their possession necessary to aid the registrars in the discharge of their respective duties.

Registration to cease.

SECT. 5. All registration of voters in said city shall cease at ten o'clock in the evening of the seventh day next preceding the day of any election; and no name shall thereafter be entered on the voting lists of said city, except as provided in section ten of chapter three hundred and seventy-six of the acts of the year eighteen hundred and seventy-four.[1] And the registrars shall, at least twenty-four days previous to the day of the annual state election, cause notices of the time of closing, together with printed lists of the voters in each ward, to be posted

---

[1] As amended by St. 1878, chap. 233. For provisions as to register of voters, see St. 1878, chap. 251.

in one or more places in such ward, with notices _{Sessions of} thereon stating the place and hours in which they _{registrars.} will hold sessions to correct and revise the lists; and such sessions shall be held in some place convenient to the voters, three or more hours daily, for at least twelve days within the twenty-four days immediately preceding the annual state election, and in addition, six evening sessions, of at least two hours length each, shall be held within the said twenty-four days.

SECT. 6.   The registrars, before entering upon the _{Naturalized} voting list the name of a naturalized citizen who is _{citizens.} an applicant for registration, shall require him to produce for their inspection his papers of naturaliza-tion, and shall be satisfied that he has been legally naturalized, and they shall also require such appli-cant to make oath that he is the identical person to whom said papers were issued; but they need not require the production of such papers after they have once examined and passed upon them.

SECT. 7.   The city council shall furnish office _{Office room.} room for the registrars, and such aid as shall be necessary for carrying out the provisions of this act.

SECT. 8.   Whoever gives a false name or a false _{False answers.} answer to any registrar concerning any matter relat-ing to the registration of voters, or to the right of any person to vote, shall incur the same penalty

which is provided by law for giving a false name or
false answer to the selectmen of towns when in
session to correct the lists of voters.

SECT. 9.   Any registrar who wilfully neglects or
refuses to perform the duties of his office shall, for
each offence, forfeit a sum not exceeding two hundred dollars.

APPROVED MAY 4, 1877.

STATUTE 1854.   CHAPTER 338.

AN ACT FOR SUPPLYING THE CITY OF WORCESTER WITH
PURE WATER.

Be it enacted, &c., as follows :

SECT. 1.   The City of Worcester is hereby authorized to hold, by purchase, and to convey to, into,
and through, the said city, the water of the Henshaw Pond, so called, in the town of Leicester, and
the waters that may flow into and from the same,
and any water-rights connected therewith, or (if the
city council shall so elect) the waters of a brook
running through the town of Holden and through
the westerly part of Worcester, called Tatnic Brook,
the water to be taken from a point in the same in
said town of Holden, about two miles above the village of Tatnic, so called, in said Worcester; and
said city may also hold, by purchase, any lands or

Water, where obtained.

May hold land, &c.

real estate, necessary for laying or maintaining an aqueduct for conducting the water from either of said sources to said city, and for forming reservoirs, and may also hold land around the margin of said pond, or around the margin of any reservoir or water source which they may possess or create, in the valley of said brook, for the purpose of furnishing a supply of pure water for the City of Worcester.

SECT. 2. The said city may make and build a permanent aqueduct, from either of the aforesaid water sources, to, into, and through, the said city, and secure and maintain the same by any works suitable therefor, may erect and maintain a dam or dams, at the outlet of said pond, or in the valley of said brook, at the point above mentioned, and at other points above the same, in the valley of said stream, to raise and retain the waters therein ; and may erect and maintain reservoirs, enlarge water sources, make and maintain public hydrants, in such places as may be deemed proper ; may distribute the water through the city, and for that purpose may lay down pipes to any house or building in the city, by consent of the owner or owners of them thereto, and may regulate the use of the water, and establish rents and prices to be paid therefor ;[1] and the city

May build aqueduct, &c.

---

[1] May establish rules and regulations, with penalty. St. 1875, chap. 150. Persons corrupting, &c. St. 1878, chap. 183; St. 1879, chap. 224; St. 1880, chap. 185.

may, for the purposes aforesaid, carry and conduct any aqueduct or other work, over or under any street, highway, or other way, or in such manner as not to obstruct the travel thereon, and may enter upon and dig up any such road, street, or way, by consent of the town in which the same may'be, for the purpose of laying down pipes beneath the surface thereof, and for making and repairing the same; *provided, however*, that nothing contained in this section shall be so construed as to authorize said city to take or flow the land, or to take, or in any way injure, the property of any person or corporation, without the consent of the owner or owners thereof.

City to appoint commissioners.

SECT. 3.   The rights, powers, and authority, given to the City of Worcester, by this act, shall be exercised by the said city, subject to the restrictions, duties, and liabilities, herein contained, in such manner, and by such commissioners, officers, agents, and servants, as the city council shall, from time to time, ordain, appoint, and direct.

City to issue scrip.

SECT. 4.   For the purpose of defraying the cost and expenses of such land, estate, water, and water-rights so purchased and held, for the purposes mentioned in this act, and of constructing said aqueduct and works necessary and proper for the accomplishment of this act, and all expenses incident thereto, the city council shall have authority, from time to time, to borrow such sum or sums of money, and to issue notes, scrip, or certificates of debt therefor, to an amount not exceeding two hundred and fifty thousand dollars, bearing interest at a rate not exceeding the legal rate of interest in this Commonwealth, the said interest to be payable semi-annually, and the principal shall be made payable at periods not more than twenty years from the issuing of said When payable. scrip, notes, or certificates, respectively; and the city council may sell the same, or any part thereof, from time to time, at public or private sale, or pledge the same for money borrowed for the purpose of this act, on such terms and conditions as the city council shall judge proper; and the city council are hereby authorized, from time to time, to appropriate, grant, and assess, such sum or sums of money, not exceeding twenty thousand dollars in any one year, towards paying the principal of the money so borrowed or obtained, and the interest thereof, in the same manner as money is appropriated, granted, and assessed, for other city purposes.

SECT. 5. The city council shall, from time to Price of water. time, regulate the price or rent for the use of the water, with a view to the payment from the net income and receipts, not only of the semi-annual interest, but ultimately of the principal of said debt so contracted, so far as the same may be practicable and reasonable.

Penalty for diverting water, &c.

SECT. 6. If any person shall wantonly or maliciously divert the water, or any part thereof, of any of the ponds, streams, or water source, which shall be taken by the city, pursuant to the provisions of this act, or shall corrupt the same, or destroy or injure any dam, aqueduct-pipe, conduit, hydrant, machine, or other property held, owned or used by the city, by the authority and for the purposes of this act, every such person or persons shall forfeit and pay to said city three times the amount of the damages that shall be assessed therefor, to be recovered by any proper action, and every such person or persons may, moreover, on indictment for and conviction of either of the wanton and malicious acts aforesaid, be punished by a fine not exceeding one thousand dollars, and by imprisonment not exceeding one year.

City to make contracts.

SECT. 7. Nothing in this act contained shall be construed to authorize said city to take or to appropriate the property of any person or corporation, to its own use, unless it be by contract or agreement with the owner thereof.

SECT. 8. The mayor and aldermen of said city

shall notify and warn the legal voters of said city, *Act void, unless accepted in sixty days.* to meet in their respective wards, on such day as the said mayor and aldermen shall direct, not exceeding sixty days from and after the passage of this act, for the purpose of giving their written votes upon the question, whether they will accept the same ; and if a majority of the votes so given upon the question shall be in the negative, this act shall be null and void.

SECT. 9.   This act shall take effect from and after its passage.

April 20, 1854.

ADOPTED BY THE VOTERS, MAY 27, 1854.

STATUTE 1856.   CHAPTER 189.

AN ACT IN ADDITION TO AN ACT TO SUPPLY THE CITY OF WORCESTER WITH PURE WATER.

SECT. 1.   The city of Worcester is hereby author- *Water, where obtained.* ized and empowered to take and convey into and through the said city the waters of Kettle Brook, so called, in the southwesterly part of said city, the waters of the same to be taken from said brook at a point about two miles from the village of New Worcester, so called, by an aqueduct, direct into said city,

or at a point higher up said brook in the town of
Leicester, and conducted by an artificial channel into
Henshaw Pond, so called, in said town of Leicester,
and so through said pond and along with the waters
of said pond into said city; or take the waters of
Half-way River, so called, in the southerly part of
Worcester, from a pond raised by means of a dam
across the valley of said river; or to take water from
Mill Brook or vicinity, so called, in the northerly part
of Worcester, or from Quinsigamond Pond, so called,
in the easterly part of said Worcester, as the city
council may elect, and to take and hold any water
that may flow into any of said ponds or streams, or
into and from either of the above water-courses, and
May hold land. any water-rights connected therewith, and any lands
or estates necessary for the laying out and maintaining an aqueduct for conducting waters from either of
said sources to said city, and for forming reservoirs;
and may also take and hold land around the margin
of either of said ponds, or around any reservoirs or
water-sources which they may possess or create, in
the valleys of said brooks, for the purpose of supplying the said city with pure water.

May build
aqueduct, &c.   SECT. 2.   The said city of Worcester may make
and build an aqueduct from either of the aforesaid
sources of supply, to, into and through the said city,
and secure and maintain the same by any works

suitable therefor; may erect and maintain a dam or dams at the outlet of either of said ponds, and across the valleys of either of said brooks, at the points above mentioned, and at other points above the same, to raise and retain the waters therein; and may erect and maintain reservoirs, enlarge and alter water-courses, make and maintain hydrants in such places as may be deemed proper; may distribute the waters through the city, and for that purpose may lay down pipes through and across any street, road or highway, or over and across lands to any buildings in said city; may regulate the use of the water, and establish and fix rents or rates for the consumption and use thereof; and for the purposes aforesaid, the city may conduct said aqueduct over, under or across, or along any street, highway, or other way, in such manner as not to obstruct travel thereon; and may enter upon and dig up any such road, street or highway, by consent of the town in which the same may be located, for the purpose of laying down pipes beneath the surface of the same, and for the repairing thereof.

SECT. 3. The rights, powers and authority given by this act, shall be exercised by the city of Worcester, subject to the restrictions, duties and liabilities herein contained, in such manner, and by such officers, servants and agents, as the city council shall from time to time ordain, appoint and direct.

City to appoint officers, &c.

SECT. 4. For the purpose of defraying the cost
of such land, water and water-rights, so taken and
held as aforesaid, and of constructing and maintaining said aqueduct, reservoirs and works necessary
for the accomplishment of the end contemplated by
this act, and all expenses incident thereto, the city
council shall have authority to borrow, from time to
time, such sums of money, and to issue bonds, notes
or certificates therefor, to be denominated on the
face thereof, Worcester Water Scrip, to an amount
not exceeding three hundred and fifty thousand dollars, bearing interest not exceeding six per cent.,
payable semi-annually, and the principal to be made

payable at periods not less than ten years from the
date thereof; and the city council may sell the whole
or any part of said scrip, from time to time, or
pledge the same for money borrowed for the purposes of this act, on such terms and conditions as it
shall deem proper. And the said city council is
hereby further authorized to grant appropriations,
and assess, from time to time, such sums of money,
not exceeding in any one year the sum of ten
thousand dollars, towards paying the principal of the
moneys so borrowed, besides a sum sufficient to pay
the interest thereof, in the same manner as moneys
are appropriated and assessed for other city purposes.

SECT. 5. To enable the city council to pay the

interest as it may accrue upon said scrip, and ulti- <small>Price of water.</small> mately the principal thereof, it shall be lawful for the said council to fix and establish the price or rate which shall be paid for the use of any part of said water, by any taker thereof in said city, and the same to alter, from time to time, as may be deemed expedient.

SECT. 6. If any person shall wantonly or ma- <small>Penalty for</small> liciously divert the waters, or any part thereof, from <small>diverting water, &c.</small> any of the ponds, brooks, reservoirs or water-sources, which shall be taken by the city pursuant to the provisions of this act, or shall corrupt the same, or destroy or injure any dam, aqueduct, conduit, pipe, hydrant or other property held and used by the city by authority and for the purpose of this act, every such person or persons shall forfeit and pay to the said city of Worcester three times the amount of the damages that shall be sustained thereby, to be recovered in any proper action ; and upon indictment and conviction for either of said acts, shall be punished by a fine not exceeding one thousand dollars, and by imprisonment in the house of correction of the county not exceeding one year.[1]

SECT. 7. All damages which may be sustained <small>Damages, how</small> by reason of the taking by said city of any of the <small>assessed and paid.</small>

---

[1] See page 63.

ponds or brooks aforementioned, or of the water
thereof, or the water-rights connected therewith, or
of diverting any portion of said water from its natural channel into other channels, or of erecting and
maintaining any dam or reservoir, or digging up any
land, street, road or highway, and entering upon the
same for laying, repairing and maintaining pipes,
conduits, hydrants, and other apparatus necessary
thereto, shall be paid by the said city of Worcester
to the individual or corporation injured; which damages shall be assessed in the same manner as is
provided in the twenty-fourth chapter of the Revised
Statutes[1] with regard to highways.

Act void, unless
accepted.
SECT. 8.   The provisions of this act shall be void
unless submitted to, and approved by, the voters of
the city of Worcester, at meetings held simultaneously for that purpose in the several wards, upon
notice duly given at least seven days before the
time of holding said meetings.

May 26, 1856.

APPROVED BY THE VOTERS, DECEMBER 12, 1871.

---

[1] See page 60 for manner of taking and damages.

STATUTE 1861. CHAPTER 118.

AN ACT IN ADDITION TO AN ACT FOR SUPPLYING THE
CITY OF WORCESTER WITH WATER.

Be it enacted, &c., as follows:

SECT. 1. In addition to the powers heretofore conferred, the city of Worcester is authorized to take and convey into and through said city the waters of East or Lynde Brook in Leicester, or of any other stream or pond in Leicester or Paxton, and to take and hold any land, and build and maintain any structures necessary for said purpose, in the manner, and subject to the liabilities and restrictions set forth in the one hundred and eighty-ninth chapter of the acts of eighteen hundred and fifty-six.[1]

Right to use water from Leicester or Paxton.

SECT. 2. If at any time the supply of water from the source first fixed upon and selected shall be insufficient for the wants of said city, the said city may by suitable works, conduct water from either of the other sources referred to in this act, or the act to which this is in addition, into the aqueduct first constructed, or into any reservoir therewith connected,

If supply is insufficient, may get water from other sources.

SECT. 3. Said city is further authorized to take and hold by purchase, any lands or rights, and

Purchase of necessary land or rights.

Manner of taking, see page 60.

interests therein, which may be necessary for the convenient accomplishment of the purposes of this act.

SECT. 4. This act shall take effect on its passage.

APPROVED MARCH 30, 1861.

STATUTE 1863. CHAPTER 72.

AN ACT IN ADDITION TO AN ACT FOR SUPPLYING THE CITY OF WORCESTER WITH WATER.

Be it enacted, &c., as follows :

City may hold and convey waters, lay pipes, and maintain necessary works.
SECT. 1. The city of Worcester is hereby authorized to take, hold and convey the waters collected and flowing from the easterly slope of Millstone Hill, so called, in said city, in and upon the land of Henry Putnam, in the best and most convenient manner and direction, over, through and across any streets, highways and lands in said city, into Bell Pond, so called, and thence into the city reservoir and aqueduct, and to lay any pipes, and build and maintain any works necessary therefor.

Damage sustained to be claimed within one year.
SECT. 2. All damage sustained by taking land or otherwise, may be ascertained, determined and recovered in the manner provided by law in case of land taken for highways ; but no proceedings shall

be commenced after the lapse of one year after the damage occurred.

SECT. 3. This act shall take effect upon its passage.

.APPROVED MARCH 11, 1863.

STATUTE 1864. CHAPTER 104.

AN ACT FOR SUPPLYING THE CITY OF WORCESTER WITH
PURE WATER.

Be it enacted, &c., as follows:

SECT. 1. The city of Worcester is hereby author- City may purchase East or Lynde Brook. ized to acquire and hold by purchase, or to take and hold, and convey to, into and through said city, the waters of East or Lynde Brook, in the town of Leicester, and any water that may flow into the same, and to acquire and hold by purchase, or to take and hold any lands or estates necessary for the laying out and maintaining an aqueduct for conduct- May hold lands and estates. ing the waters from said brook to said city, or for forming reservoirs, and may take and hold land around the margin of any water sources or reservoirs they may possess or create in the valley of said brook or elsewhere, for the purpose of supplying said city with pure water.[1]

---

1 See page 60 for manner of taking and damages.

SECT. 2. If at any time the supply of water from said East or Lynde Brook shall be insufficient for the wants of said city, the said city may take and conduct the water of Henshaw Pond in said Leicester and the waters that may flow into and from the same, or the waters of Kettle Brook, so called, in said Leicester, by suitable works, into the aqueduct first constructed from said East or Lynde Brook, or into any reservoir connected therewith.

May take waters of Henshaw Pond and Kettle Brook.

SECT. 3. The said city may make and build a permanent aqueduct from either of the aforesaid water sources, to, into and through the said city, and secure and maintain the same by any works suitable therefor; may erect and maintain a dam or dams across the valley of said brooks, or at the outlet of said pond, to raise and retain the waters therein; and may erect and maintain reservoirs, enlarge and alter water courses, make and maintain public hydrants, in such places as may be deemed proper; may distribute the water through the city, and for that purpose may lay down pipes through and across any street, road or highway, or over and across lands to any buildings in said city or in said town of Leicester; may regulate the use of the water, and establish and fix rents or rates for the consumption and use thereof, and may make and ordain all necessary rules, regulations and ordinances, to prevent the waste, misuse

May build aqueduct and erect dams, reservoirs, hydrants and lay pipes.

May regulate water rates, and establish rules for use.

and wrongful taking of said water :' and said city may, for the purposes aforesaid, carry and conduct said aqueduct over, under, across or along any street, highway or other way, in such manner as not to obstruct travel thereon, and may enter upon and dig up any such road, street or highway, for the purpose of laying down pipes beneath the surface of the same, and for the repairing thereof.

SECT. 4. The rights, powers and authority given by this act, shall be exercised by the city of Worces- ter, subject to the restrictions, duties and liabilities herein contained, in such manner, and by such officers, servants and agents, as the city council shall from time to time ordain, appoint and direct. Rights and powers granted, how exercised.

SECT. 5. For the purpose of defraying the cost of such land, water and water-rights, so purchased, taken and held as aforesaid, and of constructing and maintaining said aqueduct, reservoirs and works necessary for the accomplishment of the end con- templated by this act, and all expenses incident thereto, the city council shall have authority to bor- row, from time to time, such sums of money, and to issue bonds, notes or certificates therefor, to be de- nominated on the face thereof " Worcester water scrip," to an amount not exceeding two hundred City may borrow money for cost of construction. May issue scrip, and sell or pledge same.

---

1 See St. 1875, chap. 105; also see page 62.

thousand dollars, bearing interest at a rate not exceeding six per cent., payable semi-annually, and the
principal to be made payable at periods not more
than twenty years from the issuing of said scrip ;
and the city council may sell the whole or any part
of said scrip, from time to time, or pledge the same
for money borrowed for the purposes of this act, on
such terms and conditions as it may deem proper ;
and the said city council is hereby further authorized to grant appropriations, and assess, from time
to time, such sums of money, not exceeding in any
one year the sum of ten thousand dollars, towards
paying the principal of the moneys so borrowed, besides a sum sufficient to pay the interest thereof, in
the same manner as moneys are appropriated and
assessed for other city purposes.

May assess money for payment of principal and interest.

SECT. 6.   To enable the city council to pay the
interest as it may accrue upon the said scrip, and
ultimately the principal thereof, and for the support
and maintenance of said aqueduct, it shall be lawful
for the said city council to fix and establish the price
or rate which shall be paid for the use of any part of
said water by any taker thereof, and the same to
alter from time to time as may be deemed expedient.

Water rates, how fixed.

SECT. 7.   If any person shall wantonly or maliciously divert the waters or any part thereof, from

Penalty for wanton diversion of Water.

any of the ponds, brooks, reservoirs or water sources Penalty for corruption of waters, and injury to dams, aqueduct, etc.
which shall be purchased or taken by the city pur-
suant to the provisions of this act, or shall corrupt
the same, or destroy or injure any dam, aqueduct,
conduit, pipe, hydrant or other property, held and
used by the city, by authority and for the purposes
of this act, every such person or persons shall forfeit
and pay to the said city of Worcester three times
the amount of the damages that shall be sustained
thereby, to be recovered in any proper action ; and
upon indictment and conviction for either of said
acts, shall be punished by a fine not exceeding one
thousand dollars, and by imprisonment in the house
of correction in the county of Worcester not exceeding one year.[1]

SECT. 8. All damages that may be sustained by Damages sustained by individuals or corporations, how paid.
reason of the taking by said city of any land or of
the brooks or ponds aforementioned, or of the water
thereof, or the water-rights connected therewith, or
of diverting any portion of said water from its
natural channel into other channels, or of erecting
and maintaining any dam or reservoir, or digging up
any land, street, road or highway, and entering upon
the same for laying, repairing and maintaining pipes,

---

1 For Statute relating to corrupting water, see St. 1878, chap. 183; St. 1879, chap. 224 ; St. 1880, chap. 185. See page 62.

conduits, hydrants and other apparatus necessary thereto, shall be paid by the said city of Worcester to the individual or corporation injured, which damages shall be assessed in the manner provided in the general laws in regard to highways.[1]

SECT. 9. This act shall take effect upon its passage.

APPROVED MARCH 18, 1864.

STATUTE 1867.   CHAPTER 269.

AN ACT TO AMEND AN ACT FOR SUPPLYING THE CITY OF WORCESTER WITH PURE WATER.

Be it enacted, &c., as follows:

City council authorized to borrow money and issue bonds to be denominated Water Scrip.

SECT. I. For the purpose of defraying all costs and expenses incurred or to be incurred under the authority of chapter one hundred and four of the acts of the year eighteen hundred and sixty-four, the city council of the city of Worcester shall have authority to borrow from time to time such sums of money, and to issue notes, bonds or certificates therefor, to be denominated on the face thereof, "Worcester Water Scrip," as they shall deem necessary, to an amount not exceeding two hnudred

1 See page 60.

and fifty thousand dollars, in addition to the amount authorized by the act aforesaid, upon the same terms and conditions, and with the same authority in regard to interest, and the sale of said scrip, and the payment of the principal thereof, and the appropriation and assessment of money for the payment of the principal and the interest of the moneys so borrowed, as contained in section five of the act aforesaid.

SECT. 2. This act shall take effect upon its passage.

APPROVED MAY 24, 1867.

STATUTE 1871. CHAPTER 361.

AN ACT IN ADDITION TO AN ACT FOR SUPPLYING THE CITY OF WORCESTER WITH PURE WATER.

Be it enacted, &c., as follows:

SECT. 1. The city of Worcester may take and hold any land not exceeding ten rods in width, on and around any pond, stream or reservoir, which has been or shall be taken, held or owned by said city by authority of any of the acts for supplying said city with pure water, so far as may be necessary for the preservation and purity of the same.

City of Worcester may take land around any reservoir, etc., owned by the city.

SECT. 2. The said city shall, within sixty days from the time its city council shall vote to take any

Shall file descrip-
tion of land so
taken in registry
of deeds within
sixty days.
lands or ponds or streams of water, by authority of
this or any former act, file in the office of the registry of deeds for the county of Worcester, a description of the lands, ponds or streams of water so taken
as certain as is required in a common conveyance of
lands, and a statement of the purpose for which the
same are taken, which description and statement
shall be signed by the Mayor of said city, and the
property so taken shall vest in said city, from the
time of the filing of said description and statement.

City liable for
damages.
SECT. 3.   The city of Worcester shall be liable to
pay all damages that shall be sustained by any persons in their property by the taking of any land,
water or water-rights as aforesaid, or by the constructing of any aqueducts, reservoirs or other works
by authority of any of said acts; and if the owner of
any land, water or water-rights which shall be taken
as aforesaid, or other person who shall sustain damage as aforesaid, shall not agree with said city upon
the damages to be paid therefor, he may apply by
petition for the assessment of his damages at any
time within three years from the taking of the said
land, water or water-rights as aforesaid, and not
afterwards, to the Superior Court in the county of
Worcester.   Such petition may be filed in the clerk's
office in vacation or term time, and the clerk shall

thereupon issue a summons to the city of Worcester, returnable, if issued in vacation, to the then next
term of said court, to be held after the expiration of
fourteen days from the filing of said petition, and if
in term time, returnable on such day as the court
shall order, to appear and answer said petition ; the
said summons shall be served fourteen days at least
before the return day thereof by leaving a copy
thereof, and of the said petition, certified by the
officer who shall serve the same, with the mayor or
clerk of said city; and the court may, upon default
or hearing of the said city, appoint three commis- Commissioners
to be appointed
sioners, who shall, after reasonable notice to the to assess damages.
parties, assess the damages, if any, which such
petitioner shall have sustained as aforesaid ; and the
award of said commissioners, or of the major part of
them, being returned into and accepted by said
court, shall be final, and judgment shall be rendered
and execution issued for the prevailing party, with
costs, unless one of said parties shall claim a trial by
jury, as hereinafter provided.

SECT. 4. If either of the parties mentioned in If dissatisfied
with award, par-
the preceding section shall be dissatisfied with the ties may have a
trial by jury.
amount of damages awarded as therein expressed,
such party may, at the term at which such award
was accepted or the next term thereafter, claim in
writing a trial in said court, and have a jury to hear

and determine at the bar of said court all questions of fact relating to such damages and to assess the amount thereof, and the verdict of the jury, being accepted and recorded by the court, shall be final and conclusive, and judgment shall be rendered and execution issued thereon; and costs shall be recovered by the said parties, respectively, in the same manner as is provided by law in other civil actions in said court.

City may consent in court that a specified sum may be awarded as damages.

SECT. 5. In every case of a petition for the assessment of damages, as provided in the preceding sections, the said city may at any time after the entry thereof, offer in court and consent in writing that a sum therein specified may be awarded as damages to the petitioners; and if the petitioner shall not accept the same within ten days after he has received notice of such offer, or within such further time as the court shall for good cause grant, and shall not finally recover a greater sum than the sum so offered, not including interest on the sum recovered in damages from the date of the offer, the said city

Costs.

shall be entitled to recover its costs after said date, and the petitioner, if he recover damages, shall be allowed his costs only to the date of the offer.

Penalties for diverting water or rendering the same impure.

SECT. 6. If any person shall use any of the water which shall be taken as aforesaid, without the consent of the city of Worcester, an action of tort may be maintained against him by the city for the recovery of damages therefor; and if any person shall wantonly or maliciously divert, obstruct or retain the water, or any part thereof of any pond, brook, reservoir, or water-course, taken or held by said city as aforesaid, or shall corrupt or render impure the same, or destroy or injure any dam, reservoir, aqueduct, conduit, pipe, hydrant, machinery, or other works or property, held, owned or used by said city, by authority of any of said acts, every such person shall forfeit and pay to said city of Worcester three times the amount of the damages that shall be assessed therefor in an action of tort in the name of said city; and every such person, on indictment and conviction of either of said wanton and malicious acts, shall be punished by a fine not exceeding one thousand dollars and imprisonment in the house of correction not exceeding one year, or by imprisonment in the state prison not exceeding ten years.

SECT. 7. Nothing in this act shall be construed to authorize said city to take any pond or stream of water, or any water-rights, which said city is not now authorized by law to take. *City not to take water not now authorized by law.*

SECT. 8. This act shall take effect upon its passage.

APPROVED MAY 26, 1871.

STATUTE 1876. CHAPTER 66.

AN ACT FOR PROCURING AN ADDITIONAL SUPPLY OF PURE WATER FOR THE USE OF THE CITY OF WORCESTER.

Be it enacted, &c., as follows:

City may take water from Parson's Brook.

SECT. 1. The city of Worcester is hereby authorized to acquire and hold by purchase, or to take and hold and convey into the Hunt reservoir, for the use of the city, the waters of Parson's Brook, so called, in said city, and any waters that may flow into the same, and to acquire and hold by purchase, or take and hold any lands or estates necessary for the laying out and maintaining an aqueduct or conduit, for conducting said waters to said reservoir, or for forming and maintaining reservoirs, and may take and hold land not exceeding five rods in width around the margin of any water-courses or reservoirs they may possess or create in the valley of said brook, for the purpose of supplying said city with pure water.

May take land, etc.

To file description of land, etc., taken.

SECT. 2. The said city shall, within sixty days from the time its city council shall vote to take any lands, ponds or waters by authority of this act, file in the office of the registry of deeds for the county of Worcester, a description of the lands, ponds or waters so taken, as certain as is required in a common conveyance of lands, and a statement of the purpose for which the same are taken, which description and statement shall be signed by the mayor of said city, and the property so taken shall vest in said city from the time of the filing of said description and statement.

SECT. 3.   The city of Worcester shall be liable to Damages. pay all damages that shall be sustained by any persons in their property, by the taking of any land, water or water-rights as aforesaid, or by the constructing of any aqueducts, reservoirs or other works by authority of this act. Said damages may be recovered and paid in the manner provided in chapter three hundred and sixty-one of the acts of the year eighteen hundred and seventy-one.

SECT. 4.   The provisions of section six of said St. 1871, c. 361, chapter shall apply to all land, water and water-§ 6, to apply. rights purchased or taken, and to all works constructed under this act.

SECT. 5.   This act shall take effect upon its passage.
APPROVED MARCH 22, 1876.

5

STATUTE 1876.   CHAPTER 232.

AN ACT IN ADDITION TO AN ACT TO SUPPLY THE CITY OF WORCESTER WITH PURE WATER.

Be it enacted, &c., as follows:

May purchase waters of Kettle Brook. SECT. 1.   The city of Worcester is hereby authorized to hold, by purchase, the waters of Kettle Brook, so called, or any reservoir thereon, in the town of Leicester or Paxton, and to purchase the right to conduct the same into the Lynde Brook Reservoir in said Leicester, and to purchase any land necessary for the construction of dams or reservoirs or for the laying of pipes for this purpose.

May purchase water rights, etc. SECT. 2.   The said city is also authorized to purchase any water rights, water privileges, mills or manufacturing establishments, the lands, buildings and machinery used, owned and connected therewith, which would be injured by the diversion of the waters of said brook as aforesaid, and which are situated above the village of Trowbridgeville, in said Worcester; also, to purchase any water rights which would be affected by the diversion of the waters of said brook as aforesaid.

SECT. 3. The said city of Worcester is also au- May purchase waters of North Pond and Mill and Weasel Brooks. thorized to hold, by purchase, the waters of Mill Brook, North Pond and Weasel Brook, situated in the north part of said city; also, to purchase any land necessary for the building or maintaining of dams, reservoirs or pipes for the purpose of conducting the water of said streams and pond into said city for the use of the inhabitants thereof.

SECT. 4. The said city is also authorized to pur- May purchase mills, etc. chase any water rights, mills or manufacturing establishments with the buildings, lands and machinery used, owned and connected therewith, which may be injured by the conducting of the waters of said streams and pond into the city as provided in section three of this act; *provided*, the same are situated above the estate of the Washburn and Moen Manufacturing Company; also, to purchase any water rights which may be affected by the diversion of the waters of said streams and pond as aforesaid.

SECT. 5. This act shall take effect upon its passage.

APPROVED APRIL 28, 1876.

STATUTE 1874. CHAPTER 86.

AN ACT TO PROHIBIT FISHING IN ANY RESERVOIRS,
PONDS, AND STREAMS TAKEN BY THE CITY OF WORCESTER
FOR A SUPPLY OF PURE WATER.

Be it enacted, &c., as follows :

Fishing prohibit-
ed in waters held
by the city for
supply of pure
water.

SECT. I. No person shall take any fish from
any reservoirs, ponds and streams held or owned by
the city of Worcester for the purpose of supplying
said city with pure water, without the permission of
the water commissioners of said city, under the
direction of the city council of said city.

Penalty.

SEC. 2. Any person offending against the provisions of this act shall forfeit and pay a fine of not
less than five dollars and not more than fifty dollars,
to be recovered by prosecution before any court of
competent jurisdiction.

APPROVED MARCH 24, 1874.

STATUTE 1867. CHAPTER 106.

AN ACT CONCERNING SEWERS AND DRAINS IN THE CITY
OF WORCESTER.

Be it enacted, &c., as follows :

SECT. I. The city council of the city of Worcester may lay, make and maintain in said city all such

drains and common sewers as they shall adjudge to ^{City council may} be for the public health or convenience, and may ^{lay, and repair.} repair the same, from time to time, whenever necessary; and the said city and the citizens thereof, shall have the same rights, and be subject to the ^{Rights of} same liabilities, as if the same had been laid, made ^{citizens.} or maintained under the provisions of chapter forty-eight of the General Statutes, except as hereinafter provided.[1]

SECT. 2. The city council of said city may fix ^{City council may} the boundaries of Mill Brook, Lincoln Brook, Austin ^{fix the boundaries} Street Brook, Hermitage Brook, Piedmont Brook, ^{of certain brooks, etc.} and Pine Meadow Brook, with their tributaries; said brooks being so named as aforesaid and described in a report to the city council of said city by the committee on sewerage, on the second day of October, in the year eighteen hundred and sixty-six, and also in a plan prepared by A. C. Buttrick, copies of which report and plan are herewith presented to be filed with this act in the office of the secretary of the Commonwealth; and said city council may ^{Change and re-} alter, change, widen, straighten and deepen the ^{move obstruc-} ^{tions from the} channels of said brooks, and remove obstructions ^{same, etc.}

---

1 By St. 1878, chap. 232, sect. 2. Plans, records of changes and assessments, and other particulars, shall be kept in the clerk's office. See St. 1869, chap. 111; St. 1878, chap. 184, and 232; St. 1879, chap. 55, for general laws.

therefrom, and may use and appropriate said brooks, cover them, pave and enclose them in retaining walls, so far as they shall adjudge necessary, for purposes of sewerage, drainage and the public health.

SECT. 3. The city council of said city may take and hold, by purchase or otherwise, such land, water rights, dams, or other real estate, and so use, alter or remove the same as they shall adjudge necessary for the purposes aforesaid. And if any person shall sustain damages to his property by reason thereof, and shall fail to agree upon a settlement of the same with said city council, the same shall be assessed in the same manner and upon the same principles as damages are assessed in the laying out of highways.

SECT. 4. Every person owning real estate upon any street in which any drain or sewer may be laid under or by virtue of this act, and upon the line thereof, or whose real estate may be benefited thereby, shall pay to said city such sum as the mayor and aldermen shall assess upon him as his proportionate share of the expenditure of the city for drains and sewers; and the sum so assessed upon him shall constitute a lien upon said real estate for two years after it is assessed; and if not paid within ninety days after notice of said assessment served

City council may take and hold real estate.

Damages to be assessed as in laying out high- ways.

Persons bene- fited to pay assessment.

Assessments to constitute a lien.

upon the owner of said land, or his agent, may be
levied by a sale of said real estate to be conducted
in the same manner as a sale of real estate for the
non-payment of taxes.   And any person aggrieved Persons ag-
by the doings of the mayor and aldermen under grieved may apply for a
this section, may at any time within three months jury.
from receiving notice of any assessment, apply for
a jury in the manner provided in the sixth section
of the forty-eighth chapter of the General Statutes.[1]

SECT. 5.   For the purpose of defraying the expen- City council
ses and outlays incurred for the purposes aforesaid, authorized to issue scrip.
or so much thereof as they shall see fit, the city
council of the city of Worcester are hereby authorized
to issue, from time to time, scrip, notes, bonds or
certificates of debt, to be denominated on the face
thereof "Sewer Scrip of the City of Worcester,"
to an amount not exceeding two hundred thousand
dollars, and redeemable in not less than ten years,
from and after the date thereof.

SECT. 6.   This act shall be void unless submitted This act to be
to the voters of said city of Worcester, and approved submitted to the voters.
by a majority of those voting at ward meetings held

---

[1] May petition Superior Court, St. 1873, chap. 261.

simultaneously, in said city in the several wards, within one year from the passage of this act, which meetings shall be called in the same manner as other legal meetings of said wards, and for the purpose of voting upon the approval of this act, either solely or with other legal purposes.

APPROVED MARCH 29, 1867.

APPROVED BY THE VOTERS, APRIL 16, 1867.

STATUTE 1871.   CHAPTER 354.

AN ACT IN ADDITION TO AN ACT CONCERNING SEWERS AND
DRAINS IN THE CITY OF WORCESTER.

Be it enacted, &c., as follows :

SECT. I.   If the owner of any real estate which shall be assessed under the provisions of section four of chapter one hundred and six of the acts of the year eighteen hundred and sixty-seven, desires to have the amount of said assessment apportioned, he shall give notice thereof in writing to the mayor and aldermen of the city of Worcester, at any time before a demand is made upon him for the payment thereof; and said mayor and aldermen shall thereupon apportion the said amount into five equal parts, which apportionment shall be certified to the

Appoitionment
of assessment
under provisions
of 1867, chapter
106, § 4.

assessors of said city, and the said assessors shall
add one of said equal parts to the annual tax of said
estate each year for the five years next ensuing; Assessments to
draw interest at
and interest at the rate of seven per centum a year seven per cent.
shall be added to each of. said parts, from the time
of making the apportionment to the time such part
will become due and payable; and each of said
parts, with the interest which shall accrue thereon,
shall constitute a lien upon said real estate, in the
same manner as taxes are a lien upon said real
estate, and may be collected in the same manner as
taxes upon real estate are collected; and all assessments which shall be laid upon real estate for the
causes mentioned in said act, shall draw interest at
said rate from the time when the same became due
and payable until the payment thereof.

SECT. 2. When any assessment made under When assessment
is reduced by
authority of said act shall be reduced in amount by jury,
the verdict of a jury, the collection of the assessment so reduced may be enforced in the same manner as the original assessment might have been, if
no objection had been taken thereto; and in all
cases in which the validity or amount of any such
assessment shall be drawn in question in any suit,
the lien upon the real estate so assessed shall be
continued two years from the final determination of
such suit.

STATUTES.

Invalid assess-
ments may be
e-made.   SECT. 3. Every such assessment upon any real
estate, which is invalid by reason of any error or
irregularity in the making thereof, and which has
not been paid, or which has been recovered back,
may be re-made by the mayor and aldermen of
said city for the time being, to the amount for
which the original assessment ought to have been
made.

Costs.   SECT. 4. If any such assessment is reduced in
amount by a jury, the petititioner shall recover
costs against the respondents; if the jury shall not
reduce the amount of such assessment, the respondents shall recover costs.

Damages, how
assessed.   SECT. 5. If any person whose land, water-rights,
dams or other real estate have been or shall be
taken by said city by authority of sections one, two
or three of said act, shall not agree with said city
upon the amount of the damages to be paid therefor, he may have them assessed by the county
commissioners for the county of Worcester, by
making a written application therefor at any time
within two years of the passage of this act, or within
two years after the taking of said land, water-rights,
dams or other real estate, and not afterwards; and
if either party is dissatisfied with the doings of the
commissioners in the estimation of said damages,

such party may have them assessed by a jury;[1] and the proceedings shall be conducted and the damages shall be assessed in the same manner and upon the same principles as damages are or may be asssessed in the laying out of highways in said city.

SECT. 6. In every case of a petition for the assessment of damages, or for a jury, as provided in the preceding section, the said city may offer in court and consent in writing, that a sum therein specified may be awarded as damages to the complainant; and if the complainant shall not accept the same within ten days after he has received notice of such offer, or within such further time as the court shall for good cause grant, and shall not finally recover a greater sum than the sum so offered, not including interest on the sum recovered in damages from the date of the offer, the said city shall be entitled to recover its costs after said date, and the complainant, if he recover damages, shall be allowed his costs only to the date of the offer.

City may consent in court that a specified sum may be awarded to complainant.

SECT. 7. This act shall take effect upon its passage.

APPROVED MAY 26, 1871.

---

[1] May petition Superior Court, St. 1873, chap. 261.

STATUTE 1869. CHAPTER 390.

An Act concerning sidewalks in the city of Worcester.

Be it enacted, &c., as follows:

May establish and grade sidewalks.

SECT. 1.   The city council of the city of Worcester is hereby authorized to establish and grade sidewalks and set curbstones in such streets in said city as the public convenience may require, and construct the same with such material as the city council shall deem expedient; and may, in like manner, from time to time, re-establish, grade, reconstruct and repair such sidewalks and curbstones, and any sidewalks and curbstones heretofore established in said

May assess expense upon abutters.

city; and may assess upon the abutters on such sidewalks the whole or any part of the expense of the same, that portion of the expense not so assessed

Assessments to be a lien.

being paid by said city.   All assessments so made shall be a lien upon the abutting lands in the same manner as taxes are a lien on real estate, and may be collected in the same manner as taxes on real estate are now collected.

When to take effect.

SECT. 2.   This act shall take effect whenever the city council of said city shall accept the same.

APPROVED JUNE 12, 1869.

ACCEPTED SEPT. 20, 1869.

STATUTE 1850. CHAPTER 188.

———

An Act concerning streets and ways in the city of
Worcester.

Be it enacted, &c., as follows:

SECT. 1. When any street or way which now is Abutters to
or hereafter shall be opened, in the city of Worces- grade streets and
ter, over any private land by the owners thereof, and public use.
dedicated to, or permitted to be used by the public,
before such street shall have been accepted and laid
out according to law, it shall be the duty of the
owners of the lots abutting thereon, to grade such
street or way at their own expense, in such manner
as the safety and convenience of the public shall, in
the opinion of the mayor and aldermen of said city
require; and if the owners of such abutting lots Proceedings in
shall after reasonable notice given by the said mayor case of neglect
and aldermen, neglect or refuse to grade such street or refusal.
or way in manner aforesaid, it shall be lawful for the
said mayor and aldermen to cause the same to be
graded as aforesaid, and the expense thereof shall,
after due notice to the parties interested, be equita-
bly assessed upon the owners of such abutting lots,
by the said mayor and aldermen in such proportions
as they shall judge reasonable; and all assessments
so made shall be a lien upon such abutting lands in

Proviso.

like manner as taxes are now a lien upon real estate : *provided*, that any such grading of any street or way by the mayor and aldermen aforesaid, shall not be construed to be an acceptance of such street or way by the city of Worcester.

No street less than 40 feet.

SECT. 2.　No street or way shall hereafter be opened as aforesaid in said city,. of a less width than forty feet, except with the consent of said mayor and aldermen, in writing, first had and obtained for that purpose.

When to take effect.

SECT. 3.　This act shall take effect in thirty days from the passing thereof, unless the city council of said city shall within that time vote not to accept the same.

APPROVED APRIL 13, 1850.

STATUTE 1850.　CHAPTER 29.

AN ACT TO INCORPORATE THE WORCESTER GAS LIGHT COMPANY.

Be it enacted, &c., as follows :

Corporators.

SECT. 1,　John W. Lincoln, George T. Rice, Charles Thurber, their associates and successors, are hereby made a corporation, by the name of the Worcester Gas Light Company, for the purpose of manufacturing and selling gas, in, the city of Worcester, in the county of Worcester, with all the pow- _{Powers and} ers and privileges, and subject to all the duties, re- _{duties.} strictions, and liabilities, set forth in the thirty-eighth and forty-fourth chapters of the Revised Statutes ;

[Also,[1] to the provisions, restrictions, and conditions, of an order adopted by the city council of the city of Worcester, on the third day of May, in the year one thousand eight hundred and forty-nine, giving leave to Blake and Darracott, and their associates, to erect coal gas works in the city of Worcester, and to lay pipes for distributing the gas through the streets of said city.]

SECT. 2. Said corporation may hold such real and Real and personal estate. personal estate as may be necessary and convenient for the purpose aforesaid, not exceeding in value the sum of two hundred thousand dollars.[2]

SECT. 3. No shares in the capital stock of said Proviso. corporation shall be issued for a less sum or amount to be actually paid in on each, than the par value of the shares which shall be first issued.[3]

SECT. 4. Said corporation with the consent of the May open the ground in streets, mayor and aldermen of the city of Worcester, shall &c., with leave have power and authority to open the ground, in any of mayor and aldermen.

1 Repealed by St. 1850, chap. 237, printed on page 81,.

2 Five hundred thousand dollars. St. 1866, chap. 27 ; St. 1869, chap. 25.

3 To be one hundred dollars. St. 1869, chap. 25.

part of the streets, lanes, and highways, in said city, for the purpose of sinking and repairing such pipes and conductors, as it may be necessary to sink for the purpose aforesaid; and the said corporation, after opening the ground in said streets, lanes, or highways, shall be held to put the same again into repair, under the penalty of being prosecuted for a nuisance: *provided*, that the said mayor and alder-men, for the time being, shall, at all times, have the power to regulate, restrict, and control, the acts and doings of said corporation, which may in any manner affect the health, safety, or convenience of the inhabitants of said city.

Proviso.

City may pur-chase, &c.

[Sect. 51.   The city of Worcester, at any time hereafter, shall have the right to purchase the franchise of said corporation, by paying therefor the actual cost of the works they shall have erected, with ten per cent. interest thereon, after first deducting such amounts as may have been paid to the stockholders as dividends upon the stock.]

Sect. 6.   This act shall take effect from and after its passage.

February 19, 1850.

---

1 Repealed by St. 1850, chap. 237, printed on page 81.

STATUTE 1850. CHAPTER 237.

AN ACT IN ADDITION TO AN ACT TO INCORPORATE THE
WORCESTER GAS LIGHT COMPANY.

Be it enacted, &c., as follows :

SECT. 1. So much of the act to which this is in
addition, as is contained in the first section thereof,
after the words "thirty-eighth and forty-fourth chapters of the Revised Statutes," and also so much as is
contained in the fifth section thereof, be and the
same is hereby repealed.

Repeal of parts of original act.

SECT. 2. The said corporation shall make such
extension of their pipes, and furnish the gas in such
quantities, as the city council may from time to time
direct : *provided*, the city council shall guarantee to
said company a profit of six per cent. per annum on
such extension. The rates of charges to the city
and the inhabitants, shall not exceed the rates that
may be charged for gas of similar kind and quality,
in either of the cities of Boston, New York, or
Baltimore.

Extension of pipes by direction of city council.

Proviso.

SECT. 3. This act shall take effect on and after
its passage.

APRIL 26, 1850.

STATUTE 1851. CHAPTER 159.

AN ACT TO INCORPORATE THE WORCESTER GAS LIGHT COMPANY.

Be it enacted, &c., as follows :

Corporators.

Name.

Powers and duties.

SECT. 1. John W. Lincoln, George T. Rice, Charles Thurber, their associates and successors, are hereby made a corporation, by the name of the Worcester Gas Light Company, for the purpose of manufacturing and selling gas in the city of Worcester, with all the powers and privileges, and subject to all the duties, restrictions, and liabilities, set forth in the thirty-eighth and forty-fourth chapters of the Revised Statutes.

Real and personal estate.

SECT. 2. The said corporation may hold such real and personal estate as may be necessary and convenient for the purpose aforesaid, not exceeding in value the sum of two hundred thousand dollars.[1]

No shares to be issued at less than par value.

SECT. 3. No shares in the capital stock of the said corporation shall be issued for a less sum or amount, to be actually paid in on each, than the par value of the shares which shall be first issued.[2]

---

1 To be five hundred thousand dollars. See St. 1866, chap. 27 ; St. 1869, chap. 25.

2 To be one hundred dollars. St. 1869, chap. 25.

SECT. 4. The said corporation, with the consent Power to open ground, &c. of the mayor and aldermen of the city of Worcester, shall have power and authority to open the ground in any part of the streets, lanes, and highways, in the said city, for the purpose of sinking and repairing such pipes and conductors as it may be necessary to sink for the purpose aforesaid, and the said corporation, after opening the ground in such streets, lanes, Held to put the same in repair again. or highways, shall be held to put the same again into repair under the penalty of being prosecuted for a nuisance : *provided*, that the said mayor and Proviso. aldermen, for the time being, shall at all times have the power to regulate, restrict, and control, the acts and doings of the said corporation which may in any manner affect the health, safety or convenience of the inhabitants of the said city.

SECT. 5. The corporation hereby created shall Shall assume liabilities of assume all the liabilities of the present proprietors proprietors of present gas of the gas light works in Worcester, in relation to works, &c. the making and selling of gas.

SECT. 6. This act shall take effect from and after its passage.

MAY 15, 1851.

STATUTE 1860. CHAPTER 14.

AN ACT CONCERNING THE FREE PUBLIC LIBRARY OF THE
CITY OF WORCESTER.

Be it enacted, &c., as follows :

Donations.

SECT. 1. The city of Worcester is hereby authorized to hold the donations of Doctor John Green and
of the Worcester Lyceum and Library Association,
and to provide for the establishment and support of

Government.

a Free Public Library, to be regulated and governed
according to the provisions of the city ordinance
passed on the twenty-third day of December, in
the year one thousand eight hundred and fifty-nine,
entitled "An ordinance for the establishment of the
Free Public Library of the city of Worcester."

City council to
make appropria-
tion.

SECT. 2. The city council of said city are authorized to make all necessary appropriations for the
erection of a suitable library building, and for the
care and preservation of the library, and for the employment of the officers to be appointed in pursuance
of said ordinance. They may further appropriate
for the establishment of said library, in the year one

Amounts.

thousand eight hundred and sixty, a sum not exceeding five thousand dollars, and thereafter such further
sums as they see fit, not exceeding three thousand
dollars in each year, for the increase of the same.

SECT. 3. This act shall take effect from and after its acceptance by the city council of said city.

APPROVED FEBRUARY 2, 1860.

ACCEPTED BY THE CITY COUNCIL MARCH 26, 1860.

STATUTE 1868.   CHAPTER 195.[1]

AN ACT CONCERNING THE FIRE DEPARTMENT OF THE CITY OF WORCESTER.

Be it enacted, &c., as follows:

SECT. 1. The city council of the city of Worcester is hereby authorized to establish a fire department for said city, to consist of as many engineers, officers, engine-men and members, as the city council, by ordinance, shall from time to time prescribe.

City of Worcester may establish a Fire Department.

SECT. 2. The city council shall have authority to make such provisions in regard to the time and mode of appointment, and the occasion and manner of the removal of either officers or members; to make such requisitions in respect to their qualifications and period of service; to define their office and duty; to fix and provide for the payment of their compensation; and, generally, to make such regulations in regard to their conduct and government, and to the management and conduct of fires and persons attending at fires, subject to penalties to be prescribed

City Council to appoint and remove officers and members, and regulate generally by ordinance.

---

[1] For provisions in the charter, see pages 15, 17.

Provided

Provisos.

by ordinance, as they shall deem expedient: *provided*, said ordinances be not repugnant to the laws of the Commonwealth: and *provided, also*, that the appointment of engine-men, hose-men, hook and ladder-men, shall be made by the mayor and aldermen.

May delegate powers and duties.

SECT. 3. The powers and duties conferred and imposed by this act may be carried into effect by the city council in any manner they may prescribe, and through the agency of any person or board to whom they may delegate the same.

Repeal.

SECT. 4. The act entitled "An Act to establish a fire department in the town of Worcester," passed on the twenty-sixth day of February, in the year eighteen hundred and thirty-five, and all other acts and parts of acts in addition thereto are hereby repealed.

When to take effect.

SECT. 5. This act shall take effect upon its passage, but it shall not operate upon existing laws and ordinances. relating to the fire department of the city of Worcester, until it shall have been adopted by the city council thereof, and until said council shall have passed an ordinance establishing a fire department for said city, under the authority of this act.

APPROVED MAY 9, 1868.

ADOPTED BY THE CITY COUNCIL, SEPT. 28, 1868.

STATUTE 1875. CHAPTER 234.

AN ACT TO INCORPORATE THE WORCESTER PROTECTIVE
DEPARTMENT.

Be it enacted, &c., as follows :

SECTION 1. John D. Washburn, Charles B. Pratt, Worcester Pro-
Augustus N. Currier, Dana K. Fitch, George E. tective Department incorpora-
Kendall, and all other officers for the time being of ted.
any incorporated company or association, and any
agent doing the business of fire insurance in the
city of Worcester, who may become associated with
them and their successors, are hereby created a body
corporate, by the name of the "Worcester Protective
Department," with power to sue and to be sued, and
may hold by purchase, devise or otherwise, real and
personal property, for the use of said corporation, to
an amount not exceeding one hundred thousand
dollars, and may sell and convey any part thereof,
subject, however, to the laws of this Commonwealth.

SECT. 2. Said corporation shall have power to May maintain a
provide and maintain a corps of men, with proper corps of men
and officers.
officers, whose duty it shall be, so far as practicable,
to discover and prevent fires, and shall provide suitable apparatus to save and preserve life and property
at or after a fire; and power is hereby granted to
such corps and its officers to enter any building on

fire, or which in their judgment is immediately exposed to, or in danger of, taking fire from other burning buildings, to protect and save life and property therein, and to remove such property, or any part thereof, at or immediately after a fire ; *provided, however*, that nothing in this act shall be so construed as to lessen, in any way, the authority of the officers or members of the Worcester Fire Department, or to warrant or justify any interference with them in the performance of their duties, nor shall it in any way justify the owner of any building or personal property, in the abandonment of his property.

Department to have right of way while going to a fire.

SECT. 3.   The officers and men of the Worcester Protective Department, with their teams and apparatus, shall have the right of way while going to a fire through any street, lane or alley in the city of Worcester, subject to such rules and regulations as the city council may prescribe, and subject also to the rights of the Worcester Fire Department, and any violation of the street rights of the Worcester Protective Department shall be punished in the same manner as is provided for the punishment of violations of the rights of the fire department of the city of Boston, in chapter three hundred seventy-four of the acts of eighteen hundred seventy-three.

SECT. 4.   In the month of June, eighteen hundred seventy-five, and in the month of June in every year thereafter, there shall be held a meeting of the Annual meeting corporation hereby created, of which ten days' of the corpora-tion. previous notice shall be inserted in at least two newspapers published in the city of Worcester, at which meeting each incorporated insurance company or association doing business in the city of Worcester, whether its officers or its agents be members of this corporation or not, shall have the right to be represented by one of such officers or agents, and each organization represented at such meeting shall be entitled to one vote.

A majority of the whole number so represented, shall have the power to decide upon the question of sustaining the corps herein before mentioned, and of fixing the maximum amount of expenses which shall be incurred therefor during the fiscal year next to ensue; and the whole of such amount, or so much thereof as may be necessary, may be assessed upon the organizations belonging to this corporation, and upon all other organizations and agencies as herein before mentioned, in proportion to the several amounts of premiums returned as received by each, as hereinafter provided, and such assessment shall be collectible by this corporation in any court of law in the state of Massachusetts.

SECT. 5.   To provide for the payment of persons Payment of employees pro-vided for. employed, and to maintain the apparatus for saving life and property contemplated, this corporation is empowered to require a statement to be furnished semi-annually by all corporations, associations, under-writers, agents, or persons, of the aggregate amount of premiums received for insuring property in the city of Worcester, for and during the six months next preceding the thirtieth day of June and the thirty-first day of December of each year, which statement shall be sworn to by the president or sec-retary of the corporation and association, or by the agent or person so acting or effecting such insur-ance in said city, and shall be handed to the treasurer of this corporation, within thirty days after the time to which such terms are to be made.

Penalty for neglecting to render account. SECT. 6. It shall be lawful for the treasurer or other appointed officer of this corporation, within ten days after the first day of January, and the first day of July, in each year, by written or printed demand, signed by him, to require from every corporation, association, underwriter, agent or per-son engaged in the business of fire insurance, in the city of Worcester, the statement provided for in the last preceding section of this act; and every officer of such corporation or association, and every individ-ual, agent, or underwriter, who shall for thirty days after such demand neglect to render the account, shall forfeit fifty dollars for the use of the corporation created by this act; and he'shall also forfeit, for their use, five dollars in addition for every day he shall so neglect, after the expiration of the said thirty days; and such additional penalty may be computed and recovered up to the time of the trial of any suit for the recovery thereof, which penalty may be sued for and recovered, with cost of suit, in any court of record within this state.

SECT. 7. This act shall take effect upon its passage.

APPROVED MAY 19, 1875.

STATUTE 1869. CHAPTER 361.

AN ACT TO AUTHORIZE THE CITY OF WORCESTER AND THE TOWNS OF HOLDEN, PRINCETON, RUTLAND, BARRE, HUBBARDSTON AND GARDNER TO TAKE STOCK IN THE BOSTON, BARRE AND GARDNER RAILROAD CORPORATION.

Be it enacted, &c., as follows:

SECT. 1. The city of Worcester is hereby author- City of Worcester may take ized to subscribe to the capital stock of the Boston, stock in Boston, Barre and Gardner Railroad Corporation, an amount Barre & Gardner Railroad. not exceeding one per centum of the valuation of said city according to the valuation of the City Assessors for the year eighteen hundred and sixty-eight, and to pay for the same out of the treasury of the city,

and to hold the same as city property. And the
towns of Holden, Princeton, Rutland, Barre, Hubbardston and Gardner are hereby authorized to subscribe to the said capital stock an amount not exceeding in all five per centum of the valuation of
said towns according to the valuation of the Assessors of each of the said towns for the year eighteen
hundred and sixty-eight, and to pay for the same
out of the treasury of the town that shall so subscribe, and to hold the same as town property; and
said stock, when so subscribed and paid for, shall be
subject to the disposal of the said city and each of
said towns that shall become subscribers to said
stock under this act, for public purposes, in the same
manner as any other property it may possess : *pro-*
Proviso. *vided*, that if the city and towns aforesaid shall
become subscribers to the stock of any other railroad company under authority that has been heretofore conferred upon them, or may hereafter be
conferred upon them, by any act of the Legislature,
the whole amount of their subscription to all railroad
companies shall not exceed five per centum of the
aforesaid valuation. The total amount to be subscribed to the capital stock of said railroad corporation shall be determined at a city or town meeting
of the city of Worcester, and towns of Holden,
Princeton, Rutland, Barre, Hubbardston and Gardner, legally warned and called.

SECT. 2. The said city of Worcester, and towns May raise money by loan or tax to pay subscriptions. of Holden, Princeton, Rutland, Barre, Hubbardston and Gardner, are hereby authorized to raise by the issuing of bonds, or by loan or tax, any sums of money which shall be required to pay instalments or subscriptions to said stock and interest authorized by this act. ·

SECT. 3. The said city of Worcester, and towns Subscription. of Holden, Princeton, Rutland, Barre, Hubbardston and Gardner, may appoint a committee who shall subscribe in behalf of the city or town for such number of shares in the capital stock of said corporation as shall be voted by said city or towns. And said Vote of city, how to be cast. committee are hereby authorized to cast the vote of said city and towns in the choice of directors of said railroad at the first meeting of the stockholders thereof, after the said city or towns shall have subscribed, called for that purpose; and thereafter the vote of said city or towns in the choice of directors of said railroad shall be cast by the person or persons whom said city or towns may appoint.

APPROVED JUNE 8, 1869.

STATUTE 1871.   CHAPTER 339.

AN ACT TO AUTHORIZE THE CITY OF WORCESTER TO
ESTABLISH A CITY HOSPITAL.

Be it enacted, &c., as follows:

May establish a
City Hospital.

SECT. 1.   The city of Worcester is hereby authorized to erect, establish and maintain a hospital for
the reception of persons who, by misfortune or pov-
erty, may require relief during temporary sickness.

City Council may
make regulations
for management.

SECT. 2.   The city council of said city shall have
power to make such ordinances, rules and regulations as they may deem expedient, for the appointment of trustees and all other necessary officers,
agents and servants for managing the said hospital.

SECT. 3.   This act shall take effect upon its passage.

APPROVED MAY 25, 1871.

STATUTE 1873.   CHAPTER 282.

AN ACT TO AUTHORIZE THE CITY OF WORCESTER TO
PURCHASE LAND FOR SLAUGHTER-HOUSES.

Be it enacted, &c., as follows:

May purchase
and lease land
for slaughter-
houses.

SECT. 1.   The city of Worcester may purchase and
hold land as a place for carrying on the business of

slaughtering cattle and other animals, and may lease the same for said purpose upon such terms and conditions as the city council of said city shall prescribe.

SECT. 2.   This act shall take effect upon its passage.

APPROVED MAY 12, 1873.

STATUTE 1874.   CHAPTER 229.

AN ACT TO AUTHORIZE THE CITY OF WORCESTER TO TAKE AND HOLD LAND FOR SLAUGHTER-HOUSES AND FOR OTHER PURPOSES.

Be it enacted, &c., as follows:

SECT. I.   The city of Worcester may take and hold by purchase or otherwise, such a tract of land, within said city, bordering on the line of some railroad not within two miles of the city hall building in said city, and not exceeding three hundred acres in extent, as the mayor and aldermen of said city may adjudge necessary and suitable for the purpose of providing a place or places for carrying on the business of slaughtering cattle, sheep and other animals, and for melting and " rendering" establishments.

May take land for providing a place for slaughtering cattle, &c.

SECT. 2.   If the mayor and aldermen of said city

Damages to be
determined as
for land taken
for highways.

fail to agree with the owner or owners of said land, as to the damage to be paid therefor, such damages shall be determined and recovered in the same manner in which damages are determined and recovered for land taken for highways.

APPROVED MAY 11, 1874.

STATUTE 1880. CHAPTER 56.

AN ACT TO EXTEND THE TIME DURING WHICH THE CITY OF WORCESTER IS AUTHORIZED TO BUY AND HOLD CERTAIN LAND FOR A PUBLIC PARK AND A RESERVOIR.

Be it enacted, &c., as follows :

The city of Worcester, by its city council, at any time within two years from the fifteenth day of April, in the year eighteen hundred and eighty, may buy and hold for the purposes named in chapter one hundred and ninety-six of the acts of the year eighteen hundred and seventy-three, the land therein described.

APPROVED MARCH 5, 1880.

ORDINANCES.

CITY OF WORCESTER,

IN THE YEAR ONE THOUSAND EIGHT HUNDRED AND EIGHTY.

Be it Ordained by the Mayor, Aldermen and Common Council of the City of Worcester, in City Council assembled, as follows:

CHAPTER I.

ASSESSORS.

SECTION 1. The assessors shall hold their office for the term of three years and shall meet as soon as practicable after the annual election of an assessor in each year, and organize themselves into a board by the choice of a chairman and clerk; and a majority of the board shall be required for the transaction of business.

Organization and term of office.

SECT. 2. The clerk shall have the care and custody of all the books, papers, and documents belonging to the board, and shall deliver the same

Clerk of assessors.

Duties of. to his successor in office. He shall keep a record of all the transactions of the board, including the names of all persons whose taxes may be abated, or corrected, the amount of tax originally assessed, and the amount abated and the reasons for such abatement, in suitable books to be furnished by

To be a registrar of voters. the city. He shall be *ex-officio* a member of the board of registrars of voters.

Assessors. Duties of. SECT. 3. It shall be the duty of the assessors on the first day of May, in each year, or as soon as practicable thereafter, to assess all taxes in the manner prescribed by law; and for this purpose they may, when deemed necessary by them, call upon the assistant assessors, or any of them, for the performance of any duty relating to said assessment. They shall complete their assessment and place the list of taxes with their warrant for the collection of the same, in the hands of the collector, on or before the first day of September, in each year, and they shall indicate in said list the residence of the several persons assessed.

Duties. SECT. 4. It shall be the duty of the assessors to furnish any information in their possession necessary to aid the registrars of voters in the discharge of their respective duties.

CHAPTER II.

AUDITOR.

Charter, Sec. 18, 19.

SECT. 1. The city auditor shall give a bond with surety or sureties, to be approved by the mayor and aldermen, in the sum of five thousand dollars, for the faithful performance of his duties, and the delivery to his successor or to the city clerk, of all books, papers, documents and property belonging to said office. Whenever the office of auditor shall be vacant by death, resignation, or otherwise, or whenever he may, from any cause, be unable to perform the duties of said office, the mayor may appoint an auditor *pro tempore*, to hold office, unless sooner removed by the mayor, until the vacancy shall be filled by the city council, or the disability shall cease, as the case may be. The auditor *pro tempore* shall have all the powers and be subject to all the liabilities which pertain to the office; but no official bond shall be required of him unless the same be ordered by the mayor.

SECT. 2. The auditor shall, under the direction of the committee on finance, keep his accounts in such form, and by such divisions and in such details,

Shall give bond.

Vacancy in the office.

To keep accounts.

as may be necessary to a clear exhibit of the expenses incurred by each of the several departments of the government, in their various operations, stating, among other things, the appropriation for each department, and for each distinct object of expenditure; and, whenever the appropriations for any department or for any objects have been exhausted, he shall immediately communicate the fact to the city council, and all expenditures therefor shall cease until a further appropriation is duly made.

Furnish certain information to officers. The auditor shall, when requested, furnish to the chairman of the board, committee, or head of the department having work in charge, the amount of the appropriation therefor, and the amount drawn for in gross or in detail, when requested so to do.

To be clerk of committees.
Receive bills. SECT. 3. The auditor shall be clerk of the committees on finance and claims. He shall receive all bills and accounts from persons having demands against the city, examine them in detail, and have them filed and entered in books in such manner and form as the committee on finance may direct. All doubtful bills and accounts, so received, shall be presented by the auditor to the committee, at their next meeting, before being entered in said books.
Make reports. He shall make an exhibit of the state of the appropriations monthly to the city council, and shall

render such other service as the city council, or said committee, may direct.

SECT. 4. The auditor shall present to the city Present yearly council on the first Monday of January in each year, estimates, and a yearly report. as far as he may be able, an estimate of the amount of money necessary to be raised for the current financial year, under the respective heads of appropriations; said estimate shall state the amount of contracts unfulfilled, the probable cost of completing work commenced, and of executing orders not yet entered upon, and also the amount required by law to be applied, during the current financial year, to the liquidation of the city debt. He shall also submit, at the time aforesaid, a report showing all the receipts and expenditures of the past financial year, giving in detail the amount of appropriations and revenue, and the expenditures for each specific object, the same to be arranged to conform as nearly as may be with the accounts of the city treasurer; said report shall be accompanied by a statement of all debts or liabilities of the city, the rates of interest thereon, and the year in which the same will become due, and a schedule of all property belonging to the city, and of all leases of city property, with the rates of rents, names of tenants, and date and termination of leases. Each officer of the city, and each committee of the city council, shall furnish to the

City officers to give information to auditor.
auditor all the information in their possession that will assist him in making up the report and estimates herein called for.

Returns to assessors.
SECT. 5. It shall be the duty of the auditor, on the first day of May in each year to make a return to the assessors of all sums appropriated, granted or lawfully expended by the city since the last preceding annual assessment, and not provided for therein; and all sums necessary to satisfy final judgments recovered against the city, specifying the sums for the payment of which the city shall have voted to 'contract debts under section three of chapter two hundred and nine of the Acts of 1875; also the amount of temporary loans expressly made payable from the taxes of the current year, by vote of said city, and incurred in anticipation thereof; also all sums required for the payment of interest upon the debt of the city; also the amount of money reported to him by the commissioners of the sinking funds as required to be raised that year by taxation as the necessary contribution to each of the sinking funds of the city for the redemption of the debt to which each of said funds is applicable according to law.

Departments to return Auditor special taxes, &c.
SECT. 6. It shall be the duty of the several departments and officers of the city to cause to be delivered to the auditor, who shall take account of

and deliver the same to the city treasurer for collection, all special taxes, assessments and accounts against persons indebted to the city; and no other department or officer of the city shall receive payment of any such account, except when specially authorized to receive the same.

SECT. 7. All officers authorized to receive money in behalf of the city, except the collector of taxes, shall, as often as once in each month, pay over the same to the city treasurer, reporting at the time of payment the amount thereof to the auditor; and the auditor shall audit the accounts of all such officers at the close of each municipal year, and at the expiration of their respective terms of office, or at any other time when ordered by the city council, and for this purpose he shall have access to all books and vouchers in the possession of any officer or committee of the city, and he shall, in every case when so ordered, report to the city council the result of his examination.

City officers, shall pay money collected to treasurer monthly and report to auditor.

Auditor to audit accounts of city officers.

CHAPTER III.

BUILDING AND NUMBERING.

City council to regulate the numbering of buildings.

SECT. I. The city council shall have power to cause numbers of regular series to be affixed to or inscribed on all dwelling-houses and other buildings erected, or fronting on any street, lane, alley or public court in said city, and shall have power to determine the form, size and material of such numbers, and the mode, place, succession and order of affixing them on such houses or other buildings; and the owner, agent or person having the control of any building or part of a building, shall affix to the same the number designated by the city council or a committee thereof duly authorized, and shall not affix to the same, nor permit to remain thereon more than one day, any number contrary to the direction of the city council or committee so authorized.

CHAPTER IV.

BY-LAWS AND ORDINANCES.

By-laws to be termed ordinances.
Enacting style.

SECT. I. All by-laws passed by the city council shall be termed ordinances, and the enacting style, which shall be but once recited in each ordinance, shall be "Be it ordained by the mayor, aldermen and common council of the city of Worcester, in city council assembled, as follows : "

SECT. 2. In all votes in which either or both Form of votes. branches of the city council express any thing by way of command, the form of expression shall be " Ordered," and whenever either branch or both branches.express opinions, principles, facts or purposes, the form of expression shall be " Resolved."

CHAPTER V.

CITY DOCUMENTS.

SECT. 1. All city documents, except the rules Form and distribution of city and regulations of the police and fire departments, documents. shall be printed in pamphlet form, of uniform size, and bound together, annually, in one volume, under the direction of the city clerk, one copy of which shall be deposited in the Free Public Library ; one in the library of the American Antiquarian Society ; one in the library of the Worcester County Mechanics' Association ; one in the library of the Worcester Society of Antiquity ; and one shall be sent to the State library ; one to the Free Public Library of Boston ; and one to the Smithsonian Institute at Washington.

CHAPTER VI.

CITY HOSPITAL.

See St. 1871, c. 339, printed on page 94.

Trustees to have
entire control.

How board is
constituted.

SECT. 1.   The entire care, management and control of the city hospital shall be vested in a board of trustees consisting of seven persons, three of whom shall be selected from the members of the city council, and four from the citizens at large.

Election and
term of office.

SECT. 2.   The present board of trustees elected under the provisions of an ordinance entitled 'An Ordinance relating to the City Hospital,' passed by the city council, June 26th, 1871, shall continue in office according to the terms and conditions of said ordinance.   In the month of January, in the year eighteen hundred and eighty-one, and annually thereafter in said month, there shall be elected by concurrent vote, to be trustees of said hospital, one member of the board of aldermen, and two members of the common council, to hold their offices for one year, and one citizen at large to hold his office for four years, and until others are chosen respectively in their places.   When-

Vacancy.

ever any vacancy shall occur in said board by death, resignation, or otherwise, such vacancy shall be reported by said board to the city council.

Said trustees shall meet as soon as practicable Organization of board. after each annual election, and choose a president and secretary from their own number, and a major- Quorum. ity shall constitute a quorum for business.

SECT. 3. Said trustees shall prepare all needful Trustees to make rules. rules and regulations for the government and man- agement of said hospital. They may appoint such Appoint physi- cians, &c., and consulting and visiting physicians and surgeons as fix compensation. they shall deem expedient, and they may also appoint such subordinate agents, assistants, and domestics as they may consider necessary, and fix their compensation.

SECT. 4. Said trustees may lease suitable lands May lease land, &c., make re- and buildings for the purpose of said hospital, and pairs and buy furniture, &c. have the care and control of the same; make all necessary repairs, alterations and improvements, and purchase furniture, bedding, and such other appur- tenances as may be needful for the institution.

SECT. 5. The city hospital is established for the For what estab- lished. reception of those only who require temporary relief during sickness. The trustees may, however, admit other persons temporarily, when necessity requires ; but such persons shall be removed as soon as their condition will permit. The trustees may, when compensation therefor is made, afford separate apartments and more accommodations than those which are customary. Such extra compensation shall be credited to the appropriation for the hospital. The trustees shall present to the city council, on the first Monday of January in each year, as far as they may be able, an estimate of the amount of money required for maintaining and conducting said hospital for the current financial year. They shall also submit at the time aforesaid a report in detail of the receipts and expenditures of said hospital during the preceding financial year, together with such other matter in reference to the general state of the institution as they may judge to be of public interest. Said trustees shall not expend for any purpose a greater sum than shall be appropriated or authorized by the city council.

Trustees to present estimates to city council.

Shall report.

Shall not exceed appropriation.

CHAPTER VII.

CITY OFFICERS.

SECT. 1. The city council shall, in the month of January, annually, elect by joint ballot, in convention, a treasurer and collector of taxes, city clerk, solicitor, auditor, engineer, messenger, water commissioner, water registrar, commissioner of highways, commissioner of public grounds and shade trees, commissioner of Hope cemetery, commissioner of the Jaques fund and other funds of the city hospital, superintendent of public buildings, and superintend-' ent of sewers.

SECT. 2. The city council shall, in the month of January, annually, elect, by concurrent vote, four trustees of the city hospital.

SECT. 3. The city council shall, in the month of February, annually, elect, by concurrent vote, a pound keeper, one or more surveyors of lumber, three fence viewers, and one or more field drivers; and, in the month of February or March, in the year eighteen hundred and eighty-one, and biennially thereafter in February or March, elect, in the same manner, a registrar of voters.

SECT. 4. The city council shall, in the month of February or March, annually, elect, by joint ballot, in convention, an assessor of taxes.

Assessor.

SECT. 5. The city council shall, in the month of December, annually, elect, by joint ballot, in convention, a chief engineer of the fire department, four assistant engineers, two directors of the free public library, and two overseers of the poor.

Engineers fire department, directors of free public library, overseers of the poor.

SECT. 6. The city council shall, in the month of

Commissioner of
sinking funds.
December, annually, elect, by concurrent vote, a commissioner of the sinking funds.

City physician.
SECT. 7. The mayor, with the approval of the board of aldermen, shall, in the month of January, in the year eighteen hundred and eighty-two, and every third year thereafter, in said month, appoint a city physician.

Board of health.
SECT. 8. The mayor, with the approval of the board of aldermen, shall, in the month of January, annually, appoint a member of the board of health, to hold office for the term of two years from the first Monday in February next succeeding said appointment.

Sealer.

Inspector, &c.,
measurer, weigh-
er, undertaker.
SECT. 9. The mayor and aldermen shall, in the month of March, annually, appoint a sealer of weights and measures, an inspector of milk, one or more measurers of wood, bark and other articles, one or more weighers of hay and other articles, and one or more funeral undertakers.

Inspector of
election.
SECT. 10. The mayor and aldermen shall, in the month of October, annually, elect, for each ward of the city, an inspector of elections, who shall hold office for the term of three years from the first day of November then next succeeding.

SECT. 11. The city council shall, by concurrent Compensation of officers. vote, fix the compensation of any, or all of the above named officers, as soon as may be after their election or appointment.

SECT. 12. Any officer elected or appointed as Removal and filling vacancies. aforesaid, may be removed for cause and any vacancies occasioned by death, resignation or otherwise, shall be filled in the manner provided for the election or appointment of the officers above named.

SECT. 13. The mayor and aldermen shall, annu- Police department. ally, as soon after the organization of the city government as may be convenient, appoint a city marshal, two assistant marshals, one captain of night police, and as many policemen as in their judgment may be required, and fix their compensation.

SECT. 14. The mayor and aldermen are hereby Other officers. authorized to appoint any subordinate officer or officers, whose election or appointment is not otherwise herein provided for, that they may deem necessary for the public good, define their duties and fix their compensation.

SECT. 15. All of the officers before named, where Tenure of office. no other provision is made, shall continue in office until the regular annual election, or until their respective successors shall be chosen and qualified; except in case of removal, death, or resignation.

CHAPTER VIII.

CLERK.

City clerk,
duties of.

SECT. 1. The city clerk shall keep a book in which shall be alphabetically arranged the names of all the streets, highways and sidewalks, which now are or may hereafter be accepted or laid out in the city of Worcester, with the date of such laying out or acceptance, and the width thereof, and all alterations therein from time to time made by the city council.

St. 1878, c. 232,
§ 2.

He shall keep the plans and descriptions of all main drains and common sewers, belonging to the city, with a true record of the charges of making and repairing the same, and of all assessments therefor, and shall furnish the auditor with an account of any and all assessments made by the city council or the mayor and aldermen relating to streets, sidewalks, sewers, or otherwise, as soon as may be after such assessments are made, and perform such other duties as the city council or the mayor and aldermen may from time to time require, and shall, on or before the first Monday in January, annually, report in detail in writing, to the city council, all moneys received by him as fees or otherwise during the preceding financial year.

To be a registrar
of voters.

SECT. 2. The city clerk shall be *ex-officio* a member of the board of registrars of voters, and also keeper of the city seal.

CHAPTER IX.

COMMISSIONER OF HIGHWAYS.

SECT. 1. The commissioner of highways shall, Commissioner of highways shall have the care of streets, &c. under the direction of the committee on highways and sidewalks, have the general superintendence of the public highways, streets, sidewalks, lanes, and bridges of the city; attend to the construction, alteration, grading, paving, repairing and cleaning of the same; remove all obstructions or encroachments made thereon; make all contracts for labor, and for the purchase and sale of teams, tools or materials that may be required in the highway department, and have the care of all animals, vehicles, machinery, implements of labor, and buildings pertaining to or having relation to this department. He shall cause the public highways and streets, as soon as may be, after every snow storm, to be properly broken out, and made safe and convenient for travel.

SECT. 2. Whenever any highway, street, sidewalk Shall guard unsafe places. or bridge in said city, shall, from any cause, be unsafe or inconvenient for travellers or passengers, the commissioner of highways shall forthwith put up a suitable fence across such highway, street, sidewalk or bridge, and exclude all travellers from passing over the same; or cause the parts thereof, so ren-

8

dered unsafe and inconvenient as aforesaid, to be
enclosed by a sufficient fence or guard, which shall
be kept standing so long as the same shall remain
unsafe and inconvenient; and he shall maintain
thereon one or more lighted lanterns during every
night, so long as said fence or guard shall be
required.

Make estimates and plans of alterations.

SECT. 3. Whenever any change of grade or alteration is required to be made in any public highway,
street, sidewalk or bridge of the city, which may
occasion damage to abuttors or others, or may render the city liable to a suit or claim therefor, or
when any bridge is to be rebuilt, or other specific
work is to be done, involving an expenditure of
more than three hundred dollars, it shall be the duty
of the commissioner of highways, before commencing said work, to make or cause to be made, under
the direction of the committee on highways and
sidewalks, a full and particular estimate of the expense of such proposed repairs, alteration or work,
and the plans thereof, and to ascertain as near as

Damages.

may be the damage the abuttors or others will be
justly entitled to claim or demand of the city, in case
the proposed alteration is made or work done, and
to report such plans, with an estimate of the cost
and damage, to the city council. He shall also

Levels.

cause the level of the way or sidewalk altered to be

ascertained with reference to permanent objects in the vicinity, and such record or other evidence thereof shall be placed in the custody of the city engineer.

SECT. 4. The commissioner of highways shall, under the direction of the committee on highways and sidewalks, keep an exact account of the receipts and expenditures in his department, of the kind, quality and cost of all materials purchased by him for the city, with the names of the persons who have furnished them, and the names and wages of all the workmen employed by him, and where employed, which account shall at all times be subject to inspection by said committee. He shall deliver to the auditor an account of all sales of materials, or of labor performed by the department for individuals or other departments or corporations, and of the sums due therefor, and shall faithfully account for any money that he may at any time receive therefor.

Shall keep accounts.

Report to auditor.

SECT. 5. The commissioner of highways shall cause any roof, gutter, conductor, or water-spout, from which water can or shall be discharged, or may flow over or upon any street or sidewalk, contrary to the provisions of any ordinance of the city, to be removed, altered, or repaired, or connected with the common sewer, at the expense of the person owning

He shall remove, &c., defective water spouts.

or having the control of such roof, gutter, conductor,
or water-spout, first giving notice to the owner or
occupant, and giving ten days for such owner or
occupant to make the alterations required by this
ordinance.

He shall make
detailed reports.

SECT. 6. On or before the first Monday of January in each year he shall make to the city council a
detailed report of the work done and money expended in his department during the preceding
financial year; specifying as near as may be the
amount expended upon different streets, number of
feet of curb stones and yards of paving laid, and cost
of same, and such other information as he may consider desirable; together with an account and
appraisal of the public property under his charge;
the appraisal to be made by the commissioner and
the committee on highways and sidewalks, or a sub-
committee chosen from their number. The commissioner of highways shall also make a quarterly report
to the city council of the expenditures for each
quarter.

CHAPTER X.

COMMISSIONERS OF HOPE CEMETERY.

SECT. 1. The commissioners of Hope Cemetery shall hold their office for the term of five years, and shall meet as soon as practicable after the election of a commissioner in each year, and organize themselves into a board by the choice of a chairman and secretary of their own number; and a majority of said board shall be required for the transaction of business, and said commissioners shall make an annual report to the city council as provided in the charter of the city.

Term of office and organization of commissioners.

SECT. 2. The secretary shall have the care and custody of all books, records, papers and documents belonging to the board, and shall record all the doings of said board in a book to be furnished by the city; and he shall deliver said books, records, papers and documents to his successor in office.

Duties of secretary.

CHAPTER XI.

COMMISSIONERS OF THE JAQUES FUND AND OTHER FUNDS
OF THE CITY HOSPITAL.

Commissioners to have care of the property and receive no compensation.

SECT. 1.   The entire care, management and control of all the property, real, personal or mixed, which has been received, or shall hereafter be received, directly or indirectly, by gift, bequest or otherwise, for the benefit of the city hospital, shall be vested in a board of three commissioners, who shall serve without compensation, to be known and styled, the commissioners of the Jaques fund, and other funds of the city hospital.

Present trustees.

SECT. 2.   The persons elected, under the provisions of an ordinance entitled "An ordinance to establish a Board of Commissioners of the Jaques fund and other funds of the City Hospital," passed by the city council, October 15th, 1877, shall continue in office according to the terms and conditions of said ordinance.

Elections, vacancies.

SECT. 3.   In the month of January, in the year eighteen hundred and eighty-one, and annually thereafter, in said month, there shall be elected one member of said board, to hold office for the term of three years.   Whenever any vacancy shall occur in said board by death, resignation or otherwise, such vacancy shall be reported to the city council. Said commissioners shall meet as soon as practicable after each annual election, and choose a president and secretary from their own number, and a majority shall constitute a quorum for business.

Organization, quorum.

SECT. 4. Said commissioners shall invest, from time to time, all moneys which shall hereafter be derived from the sale of real estate or personal property, given, granted or bequeathed for the benefit of said city hospital, in the same securities and in the same manner provided by the statutes of this commonwealth for the management and investment of deposits in savings banks; excepting, however, that no part of said money or property shall be invested in the bonds, scrip or other obligations of the city of Worcester.

Investments.

SECT. 5. Said commissioners shall pay over to the city treasurer, quarterly, between the first and fifteenth days of January, April, July and October, in each year, all moneys received as income from any property heretofore or hereafter granted, bequeathed, or conveyed, for the benefit of the city hospital, whether as rents, interest or otherwise, unless conditions are connected with the bequest or gift inconsistent therewith, after deducting such sums

Net receipts, disposition of.

as may be expended by them in necessary repairs
upon the property, and such sums as may be otherwise necessarily expended by them in the performance of their duties, and said treasurer's receipt
therefor shall be a sufficient voucher for such payments; all sums so paid to the treasurer shall be
credited to an account to be called the hospital fund,
and shall be used for the support and maintenance
of the city hospital and for no other purpose, and
said sums shall be paid by the city treasurer for said
purpose upon the draft of the mayor, countersigned
by the auditor in the same manner as other moneys
are paid for the support and maintenance of the
hospital.

May sell real estate.

SECT. 6.   Said commissioners, in the execution
of their trust under this ordinance, shall have full
power and authority to negotiate and make sale of
any real estate now held by the city for the use and
benefit of the city hospital, and all real estate which
shall be hereafter granted, conveyed or bequeathed
to the city for the use and benefit of said city hospital, unless conditions are connected with the bequest
or gift inconsistent therewith, and all real estate
which may at any time become the property of the
said city through any investments made by authority
of this ordinance, and for the time being not in use
for hospital purposes, in such quantities, at such

times and upon such terms as they shall regard most advantageous to the interests of all parties interested in said funds; and all conveyances of real Conveyances. estate so sold shall be executed by the mayor, under the seal of the city, and assented to in writing by said commissioners.

SECT. 7. Said commissioners shall, on the first Shall report to city council. Monday of January in each year, make to the city council a full report of their doings under the several provisions of this ordinance, for the year ending November thirtieth next preceding, and shall also state the condition of the trust funds on that date.

SECT. 8. All money, property and estate given General bequests. or bequeathed to the city for the use of the hospital, unless the donors thereof shall have otherwise directed, shall constitute a permanent fund, the principal of which shall not be diminished, and the income of which shall be devoted to the uses of the hospital.

CHAPTER XII.

COMMISSIONERS OF PUBLIC GROUNDS AND SHADE TREES.

Term of office of commissioners.

Organization.

Quorum.

Reports.

SECT. 1. The commissioners of public grounds and shade trees shall hold their office for the term of three years. They shall meet as soon as practicable after the election of a commissioner in each year, and organize themselves into a board by the choice of a chairman and secretary from their own number; and a majority of said board shall be required for the transaction of business. Said commissioners shall make an annual report to the city council as provided in the charter of the city.

Secretary, duties of.

SECT. 2. The secretary shall have the care and custody of all books, records, papers and documents belonging to the board, and shall record all the doings of said board in a book to be furnished by the city; and he shall deliver said books, records, papers, and documents to his successor in office.

CHAPTER XIII.

CONSTABLES.

SECT. 1. The mayor and aldermen may appoint such number of constables for the service of civil precepts as they shall deem proper; who shall be qualified by giving bonds according to law, and who shall be entitled to all fees received by them for service of civil processes; but all fees received by them for services in criminal cases shall be paid into the city treasury.

Constables, appointment of, bonds and fees.

CHAPTER XIV.

CONTRACTS.

SECT. 1. No contract involving the creation of an obligation against the city exceeding the sum of one hundred dollars shall at any time be made, except in pursuance of a vote of the committee charged with the supervision of the department to which the same relates, which vote shall thereupon be recorded, by the clerk of said committee; and the record of every such vote shall, at all times, be open to the inspection of the mayor, and of the members of the city council.

Contracts to be made pursuant to vote of committee.

SECT. 2.   Before making any contract for the furnishing of labor or materials, or both, for, or in
behalf of the city, involving the expenditure of more
than five hundred dollars, the committee having
charge of the same shall, when necessary, prepare,
or cause to be prepared, the requisite plans and
specifications of the work to be done.

Committee to have plans and specifications prepared.

SECT. 3.   In cases where competitive bids are
solicited by a committee for a contract with the city,
no proposal shall be received by the said committee
unless the same is sealed; and no proposals shall be
opened except in committee actually assembled;
nor shall the contents of any proposal be made
known to any person not a member of the committee until after a contract shall have been made;
provided always, that if any such proposals shall be
offered by persons who, in the judgment of said
committee, are incompetent to perform their contracts in a workmanlike manner, or are irresponsible
in respect to their means of faithfully executing the
same, the said committee may, in their discretion,
reject any such proposal, notwithstanding the same
may be at a lower rate than other proposals offered
for the same work.

Competitive bids.

SECT. 4.   In all cases where the amount of any
contract shall exceed one thousand dollars, the

*Contracts exceed-
ing one thousand
dollars.*

contract shall be in writing, and shall be signed by the mayor and a majority of said committee on the part of the city, and, after being signed by the parties, no such contract shall be altered in any particular, unless a majority of the said committee shall signify their assent thereto in writing, under their respective signatures, indorsed on said contract and approved by the mayor ; and said contract, or a certified copy thereof, shall be deposited with the auditor within forty-eight hours from the date thereof.

SECT. 5.   The city council, whenever they shall deem it expedient, may, by a special order, author- ize the expenditure of money, or the creation of an obligation against the city, without any of the form- alities before specified.

Contracts, &c., may be specially authorized.

SECT. 6.   In every contract entered into on behalf of the city, and involving the employment of me- chanics or laborers by the contractor, or furnishing of materials, a provision shall be inserted to the effect that the committee, board or other authority making such contract may, if it deems it expedient to do so, retain, out of any amounts due to such contractor, sums sufficient to cover any unpaid claims of mechanics or laborers for work or labor performed, or materials furnished under such contract, provided

Contracts shall allow city to re- tain sums to cover certain claims.

that notice in writing of such claims, signed by the claimants, shall have been filed in the office of the city clerk prior to the completion of said contract.

CHAPTER XV.

DEEDS.

Deeds, lease, &c., execution of.

SECT. 1. All deeds, leases, indentures, or conveyances under seal, that may be given or require to be executed by the city, shall be signed by the mayor and sealed with the common seal of the city.

Mortgages, redemption of.

SECT. 2. Whenever any person having lawful authority to redeem any property mortgaged to the city shall pay to the city treasurer the amount due and payable by such mortgage, the city treasurer shall report the same in writing to the mayor and aldermen; and the mayor shall, with the approbation of the board of aldermen, relieve, discharge or assign said mortgage without recourse to or liability of the city, and shall execute any deed or legal instrument that may be appropriate for such purpose. The treasurer shall also report the amount of such payment, in writing, to the auditor.

CHAPTER XVI.

DOGS.

SECT. 1. Whoever owns or keeps, or permits or allows to be kept on his or her premises, in the city of Worcester, a dog, shall, before permitting such dog to go at large or loose in said city, obtain a license therefor from the mayor and aldermen, or from some person by them authorized to grant such license, and pay to the city clerk one dollar, which shall be in addition to any sum required by the general laws of the commonwealth; and said license shall expire on the first day of May next thereafter.

Dogs to be licensed.
St. 1867, c. 130.
G. S. c. 88, § 67.

SECT. 2. On complaint being made to the city marshal of any dog within said city, whether owned or kept, or permitted or allowed to be kept, by virtue of any license duly granted under provision of this chapter, or not, which shall, by barking, biting, howling, or in any other way or manner, disturb the quiet of any person or persons whomsoever, said marshal shall forthwith give notice thereof to the person owning, keeping, permitting, or allowing upon his or her premises such dog to be kept, and such person shall thereupon forthwith cause such dog to be removed and kept beyond the limits of said city, or destroyed; and in case such

Disturbing people.
G. S. c. 88, §§ 6, 7.

dog is again found at large in any street, highway,
or public place in said city, any person may, and
every constable and police officer shall, cause such
dog to be killed and buried.

To be muzzled
when ordered.
St. 1877, c. 167. SECT. 3. The mayor and aldermen may order
that any dog or dogs, within said city, shall be
muzzled or restrained from running at large during
such time as shall be prescribed by such order.
After passing such order and the publication of the
same by posting a certified copy thereof in two or
more public places in the city, or by publication thereof once in a daily newspaper, published in said city,
said mayor and aldermen may issue their warrant
to one or more of the police officers or constables
of said city, who shall, after twenty-four hours from
the publication of such notice, kill any or all dogs
found unmuzzled or running at large contrary to
such order.

Owner refusing
to obey order.
St. 1877, c. 167,
§ 7. SECT. 4. The mayor and aldermen may cause
special service of any order passed by them to be
made upon any person, requiring that any dog
owned or kept by such person shall be muzzled
or restrained from running at large, by causing a
certified copy of such order to be delivered to him.
Any person who, after receiving such certified copy,
shall refuse or neglect, for the period of twelve

hours after receiving such notice, to muzzle or restrain such dog as required by such order, shall pay a fine not exceeding twenty dollars.

SECT. 5. Whoever kills and buries a dog Killing dogs. according to the provisions of this chapter shall receive therefor the sum of one dollar, to be paid from the city treasury.

CHAPTER XVII.

ENGINEER.

SECT. 1. The city engineer shall have the charge Engineer, duties of. and custody of all plans of streets, sidewalks and water pipes belonging to the city; he shall enter in a book to be kept for the purpose the names of all the streets which shall be accepted, laid out and established by the city council, with the boundaries and admeasurements thereof, the names of the owners of the land, if known, over or through which such streets or ways are located, and the estates bounding and abutting thereon, and shall keep a record of all sidewalks that now are or hereafter may be laid out and established by the city council, the width, height and grade of the same, stating the boundaries and admeasurements thereof, with the date of such

9

laying out, and the names of the owners of the adjacent estates at the time when such sidewalks were established. He shall visit all dams and reservoirs belonging to the city at least once in three months. He shall, annually, on or before the twentieth day of December, report to the committee on water the amount expended on the work under his direction, and make such suggestions in relation to the works and transmit such other information in regard to them as he may think advisable.

Engineer, duties of. SECT. 2. The city engineer shall make the plans for, and shall have the supervision of, all dams, bridges, or other engineering structures that may be built by the city; he shall act as clerk to the committees on highways and sidewalks, sewers, and lighting streets, and, by himself or his assistant, for whom he shall be responsible, shall make all surveys, admeasurements, levels, and estimates, and perform such other duties as may be required of him by the mayor and aldermen, or by any committee of the city council or of either board thereof.

CHAPTER XVIII.

FENCE VIEWERS.

SECT. 1. The fence viewers of the city of Worcester shall keep a record of all their official business, which record shall be at all times open to the inspection of the mayor and aldermen or of any person by them authorized to make such inspection. Fence viewers to keep a record.

———

CHAPTER XIX.

FINANCE COMMITTEE.

SECT. 1. There shall be elected in the month of January, annually, by ballot, in each board of the city council, a joint standing committee on finance, consisting of two on the part of the board of aldermen, and three on the part of the common council. The mayor and the president of the common council shall be members of said committee *ex-officio*. Finance committee, how constituted.

SECT. 2. Said committee shall meet once a month, and as much oftener as they may deem expedient. They shall consider and report on all subjects relating to the finances of the city, and, Duties of the committee.

under direction of the city council, negotiate all loans in behalf of the city; said committee shall examine, and, if there be no objections, approve all bills and accounts against the city which have been certified by the auditor, and decide what disposition shall be made of all doubtful bills or accounts presented to them by him.

Money, how paid.   SECT. 3.   No money shall be paid out of the city treasury, except by order of the city council, or to satisfy final judgments against the city, unless the expenditures, or the terms of the contract, shall be approved or certified by the chairman of the board, or committee, or by the head of the department authorized to incur the expenditure or make the contract; nor unless the same shall be approved by the committee on finance, and drawn for by the mayor; *provided, however*, that in all cases where it may be necessary for money to be paid in advance for contracts made, or for work begun and not completed, the mayor may draw upon the city treasurer for any sum not exceeding three hundred dollars, without the approval of the committee; which draft shall be paid by the city treasurer, provided the same be countersigned by the auditor.

Accounts, how kept.   SECT. 4.   The books and accounts of the several departments shall be kept under the direction of the committee on finance, who shall determine the mode in which all bills and accounts against the city shall be certified or vouched. Said committee shall ex- Committee to examine, audit and settle the accounts of the city and securities. treasurer, for the preceding financial year; and shall not only compare said accounts with the vouchers thereof, but shall ascertain whether all sums due to the city have been collected and accounted for; they shall also examine the notes, bonds and other securities belonging to the city, and make a full and particular report of their proceedings to the city council.

SECT. 5. No expenditure shall be incurred for Clerical labor. clerical labor in the various departments of the city, nor shall any person be employed in such labor, without the concurrence of the committee on finance.

CHAPTER XX.

FIRE ARMS.

SECT. 1. No person shall fire or discharge any Fire arms not to be discharged. gun, pistol, or other firearms, that shall be loaded with ball, or shot, or with powder only, in or across any of the streets, highways or public squares, or near any dwelling house within the city; *provided*, that this section shall not apply to the use of such weapons at any military exercise or review under the authority of a commissioned officer of the militia, or in the lawful defence of the person, family or property of any citizen, or in the performance of any duty required by law, nor to any person firing a salute of cannon or artillery by leave of the mayor or committee on military affairs.

CHAPTER XXI.

FIRE DEPARTMENT.

See St. 1868, c. 195, printed on page 85.

Fire department,
how constituted.

SECT. 1. The fire department of the city of Worcester shall consist of a chief engineer, four assistant engineers, and as many engine-men hosemen, hook and ladder men and other persons, to be divided into companies, as the number of engines, and the number and quantity of other fire apparatus in service belonging to the city, shall from time to time require.

Engineers, organization of.

SECT. 2. The engineers, shall, on or before the first Monday of January in each year, organize themselves as a board of engineers by choosing a clerk by ballot. They may make such rules and orders Government of for their government as a board of engineers, and engineers, rules for fire depart- such rules and regulations in addition to this ordi- ment. nance for the better government, discipline and good order of the department, and for the extin- guishment of fires, as they may from time to time think expedient, subject to the approval of the mayor and aldermen.

SECT. 3. Whenever it shall be adjudged at any Buildings, how demolished at fire, by three or more of the engineers, of whom the fires. chief, if he be present, shall be one, to be necessary, in order to prevent the further spreading of the fire, to pull down or otherwise demolish any building, the same may be done.

SECT. 4. It shall be the duty of the chief Combustibles, how removed. engineer to inquire for and examine into all shops and other places where shavings or other combusti- ble materials may be collected and deposited, to be vigilant at all times in taking care of the removal of the same, whenever, in his opinion, the same may be dangerous to the security of the city from fires, and to direct the tenant or occupant of said shops or other places to remove the same; and in case such tenant or occupant shall neglect or refuse so to do, to cause the same to be removed at the expense of such tenant or occupant.

Dangerous build-
ings.

SECT. 5. It shall be the duty of said chief engineer to take cognizance of any building, part of a
building, or other structure, which in his judgment
may, from any cause, be dangerous by reason of fire,
and to report the same to the superintendent of
public buildings.

Chief engineer to
report.

SECT. 6. The chief engineer shall, annually, in
the month of January, report to the city council the
condition of the department, the number of men
therein and their names, the names of all .members
who have been dismissed or discharged during the
year, and such other information as the committee
on the fire department may direct.

Badges and uni-
forms.

SECT. 7. The engineers, officers and members of
the several companies regularly appointed, shall
wear such caps, badges, or insignia of office, when
on duty, as the board of engineers may from time to
time direct, and no others, to be furnished at the
expense of the city; and no other person or persons
shall wear the same at any time, except under such
restrictions and regulations as the said engineers
may direct, and all members of this department who
are employed during all the time therein shall wear
a uniform such as the board of engineers may
prescribe.

Attendance at
fires.

SECT. 8. Whenever any fire occurs out of the

city it shall be the duty of only such engineers to repair thither as shall have been designated by the chief engineer.

SECT. 9. The chief engineer shall have the sole command at fires over all other engineers, all officers and members of the fire department, and all other persons who may be present at fires; and shall direct all proper measures for the extinguishment of fires, protection of property, preservation of order and observance of the laws, ordinances and regulations respecting fires. It shall be the duty of said chief engineer to examine into the condition of all property belonging to the city and used by the fire department, and, under the direction of the com-. mittee on the fire department, to cause the same to be kept in good condition and repair; to inspect the companies attached to the said department, as often as circumstances may render it convenient, or whenever directed so to do by the said committee, and to keep, or cause to be kept, such records, rolls and other books as said committee may from time to time order.

Chief engineer, duties of.

SECT. 10. The chief engineer shall have power to suspend any officer or member of the department for insubordination or disorderly conduct, and unless such officer or member shall have been previously

Suspension of members.

10

re-instated by said chief engineer, he shall report
such suspension to the board of engineers at their
next meeting.

Supplies.

SECT. 11. All supplies for the use of the department shall be drawn by a requisition upon the chief
engineer.

Rank when chief
is absent.

SECT. 12. In the absence of the chief the assistant engineer next in rank shall act with full powers;
and seniority in rank, and all questions relative
thereto, shall be determined by the mayor and
aldermen.   .

Clerk, duties of.

SECT. 13. The clerk of the board of engineers
shall perform such duties as the mayor and aldermen or chief engineer may from time to time direct;
and also such other duties as the board of engineers
by their rules and orders may from time to time
determine. He shall have the care and custody of
all books, records, papers and documents belonging
to the board, and he shall deliver the same to his
successor in office.

Companies, num-
ber of.

SECT. 14. As many engine, hose, and hook and
ladder companies, and of such number of men, shall
from time to time be formed by the board of engineers as the committee on the fire department may

deem necessary, *provided*, however, that the appointment of engine men, hose men and hook and ladder men shall be made by the mayor and aldermen.

SECT. 15. Every company using a steamer shall Officers. have a foreman and an assistant foreman, an engineer and an assistant engineer; hose, and hook and ladder companies shall have a foreman and an assistant foreman. These officers shall be appointed in the month of December, annually, by the board of engineers, subject to the approval of the mayor and aldermen.

SECT. 16. The foremen of the several companies Foremen, duties shall, before entering upon their duties, be sworn to of. the faithful performance thereof. They shall make monthly returns to the clerk of the board of engi- Members neers of all absences of the members of their respec- derelict. tive companies from fires, or fire alarms, and if it shall appear that any member has failed to perform his duties satisfactorily to the board of engineers, no compensation shall be allowed him for such. length of time as he may have been delinquent; and if any foreman shall make a false report he shall be expelled from the department, and any pay that may be due him at the time shall be forfeited to the city. They shall also keep fair and exact rolls, specifying the time of admission and discharge of each member, with their age and residence, and accounts of all the city property intrusted to the care of the several members, in a book provided for that purpose by the city; which rolls or record books shall always be subject to the order of the board of engineers, the mayor and aldermen, or the committee on the fire department. They shall also make, to the chief engineer, true and accurate returns of all the members and the apparatus intrusted to their care, whenever called upon so to do. They shall have the care and custody of all books, records, papers and documents belonging to the company, and shall record all the doings of the company in a book furnished by the city; and they shall deliver said books, records, papers and documents to their successors in office.

Absences.

SECT. 17. For every absence at any roll-call there shall be deducted from the pay of the absent member the sum of one dollar.

Discipline.

SECT. 18. Any member of the fire department who shall wilfully neglect or refuse to perform his duty, or shall be guilty of disorderly conduct or of disobedience to his superiors in office, shall, for such offence, be dismissed from the department; and any member of the fire department may, at any time, be removed or dismissed from the department, or deposed from any office that he may hold therein, by the board of engineers.

SECT. 19. In all cases of removal from office, or **Re-instating persons removed.** from the department, by the board of engineers, the name of the person removed, with a statement of the reasons therefor, shall be transmitted to the board of aldermen at their next regular meeting, and no officer who may have been dismissed or removed from the fire department shall be reinstated therein, unless by vote of the board of engineers, concurred in by the mayor and aldermen.

SECT. 20. No company shall draw water from **Reservoirs and apparatus, use of.** the reservoirs, except in case of fire, unless by special permission of the chief engineer, nor shall any engine, hose, hook or ladder be taken to a fire out of the city, without permission of an engineer; nor shall any apparatus of the fire department be taken from the city other than to a fire, without permission from the mayor and aldermen.

SECT. 21. There shall be paid to each member **Compensation.** of the department such sum, in semi-annual payments, as the city council may from time to time determine, less the amount of fines imposed for non-attendance at fires and at roll-call; and any

member of the fire department who shall perform
the duties for a less term than one year shall be
paid pro rata for the number of months he may
have been in service.

Interference with
members, and
acting without
authority.

SECT. 22. No person shall insult, menace, hinder, obstruct, oppose, or without authority give an
order to an engineer, or fireman while on duty, nor
shall any person presume to act as a member of any
company belonging to the fire department of the
city of Worcester until he has been duly appointed
and qualified.

Municipal year.

SECT. 23. The municipal year of the fire department shall begin on the first Monday of January
annually, at 6 o'clock P. M.

CHAPTER XXII.

FIRE LIMITS, AND CONSTRUCTION OF BUILDINGS
THEREIN.

Charter, § 20, St. 1872, c. 243.   For Statute regulations, see St. 1877, c. 214.
St. 1880, c. 181, 197.

Fire limits estab-
lished.

SECT. 1. For the purpose of securing the prevention of fire in the city of Worcester, a Fire
District is hereby established therein, the boundaries
of which shall be as follows, to wit:

Beginning at a point on Main street, one hundred
and fifty feet southwesterly of LaGrange street;
thence running southeasterly parallel with and one
hundred and fifty feet southwesterly of LaGrange
street to a point one hundred and fifty feet easterly
of Southbridge street; thence northerly parallel
with and one hundred and fifty feet easterly of
Southbridge street to a point one hundred and fifty
feet southerly of Madison street; thence southeasterly parallel with and one hundred and fifty feet
southerly of Madison street to a point one hundred
and fifty feet southeasterly of Gold street; thence
northeasterly parallel with and one hundred and
fifty feet southerly of Gold street to a point one
hundred and fifty feet westerly of Washington
street; thence easterly at right angles with Washington street to a point one hundred and fifty feet
easterly of Washington street; thence southerly
parallel with and one hundred and fifty feet easterly
of Washington street to a point one hundred and
fifty feet northerly of Lamartine street extended;
thence easterly at right angles with Washington
street to the new channel of Mill Brook, as laid out
by the City Council; thence northerly by the centre
of said channel to the centre of Green street; thence
easterly at right angles with Green street one hundred and fifty feet; thence northerly parallel with
and one hundred and fifty feet easterly of Green

street to a point one hundred and fifty feet southerly of Winter street; thence easterly parallel with
and one hundred and fifty feet southerly of Winter
street to the centre of Grafton street; thence northeasterly at right angles with Grafton street, five
hundred feet; thence northerly in a straight line to
the intersection of Shrewsbury street and East
Worcester street; thence northerly at right angles
with Shrewsbury street to a point one hundred and
fifty feet northerly of Shrewsbury street; thence
southwesterly parallel with and one hundred and
fifty feet northerly of Shrewsbury street to a point
one hundred and fifty feet easterly of Summer
street; thence northerly parallel with and one hundred and fifty feet easterly of Summer street to a
point one hundred and fifty feet southerly of Belmont street; thence easterly parallel with and one
hundred and fifty feet southeasterly of Belmont
street to the centre of Hanover street; thence
northerly by the centre of Hanover street to a point
one hundred feet northerly of the north line of
Belmont street; thence westerly parallel with and
one hundred feet northerly of the north line of
Belmont street to a point one hundred and fifty
feet easterly of Lincoln street; thence northerly
parallel with and one hundred and fifty feet easterly
of Lincoln street to a point one hundred and fifty
feet southerly of Kendall street; thence westerly in

a straight line to the intersection of Salisbury street
and Grove street; thence southwesterly in a straight
line to a point one hundred and fifty feet northerly
of Highland street, opposite Harvard street; thence
westerly parallel with and one hundred and fifty
feet northerly of Highland street, one hundred and
fifty feet; thence southerly parallel with and one
hundred and fifty feet westerly of Harvard street to
a point one hundred and fifty feet northerly of
Bowdoin street; thence westerly parallel with and
one hundred and fifty feet northerly of Bowdoin
street, until it meets a line drawn parallel with and
one hundred and fifty feet westerly of Chestnut street
extended; thence southerly parallel with and one
hundred and fifty feet westerly of Chestnut street
extended; thence southerly parallel with and one
hundred and fifty feet westerly of Chestnut street
to a point one hundred and fifty feet northerly of
Pleasant street; thence westerly parallel with and
one hundred and fifty feet northerly of Pleasant
street until it meets a line drawn parallel with and
one hundred and fifty feet westerly of Irving street
extended; thence southerly parallel with and one
hundred and fifty feet westerly of Irving street to a
point one hundred and fifty feet northerly of
Chandler street; thence westerly parallel with and
one hundred and fifty feet northerly of Chandler
street to a point opposite the intersection of

11

Chandler street and Wellington street; thence southerly to the intersection of Chandler street and Wellington street; thence southwesterly at right angles with Wellington street one hundred and fifty feet; thence southeasterly parallel with and one hundred and fifty feet southwesterly of Wellington street to a point one hundred and fifty feet northwesterly of Main street; thence southwesterly parallel with and one hundred and fifty feet northwesterly of Main street to a point one hundred and fifty feet southwesterly of Piedmont street; thence southeasterly parallel with and one hundred and fifty feet southwesterly of Piedmont street to Main street; thence northerly by Main street to the point of beginning.

Wooden buildings prohibited.

SECT. 2. No wooden or frame building shall hereafter be erected within the fire district established by the preceding section.

Buildings, how constructed.

SECT. 3. The external and party walls of all buildings hereafter erected within said district shall be built of brick, stone, iron, or other hard and non-combustible material. All such walls, when constructed of brick, stone, or other similar substance, shall be properly bonded and solidly built with mortar or cement, and shall not be less than eight inches thick. The roofs of all such buildings shall be properly and securely covered with slate, tin, or other non-combustible roofing material.

SECT. 4. Except as provided in the following section, no building now erected, or hereafter to be erected within said district, shall be altered, raised, roofed, enlarged, or otherwise added to or built upon, unless the external walls and roof of the new or added parts shall be built according to the requirements of section three of this ordinance. *Altering buildings.*

SECT. 5. The board of aldermen of said city may grant licenses to make wooden additions to wooden buildings now existing within said district, upon such terms and conditions and subject to such limitations and restrictions as they may prescribe ; but before any such license is granted a notice of the application therefor shall be published three times successively in a daily newspaper in said city. *Additions.*

SECT. 6. No wooden building -shall be moved from one lot to another lot in the said district, nor from without said district into the same. *Moving to other lots.*

SECT. 7. No wooden building shall be moved from place to place on the same lot within said district without a special license being first obtained therefor from said board of aldermen. *Moving, not off the lot.*

Mills, &c., out-
side the district.

SECT. 8. No building hereafter erected in said city without said district shall be used or occupied as a machine shop or mill, or for mechanical or manufacturing purposes, unless the external walls and roof thereof shall be built according to the requirements of section three of this ordinance, without a special license being first obtained therefor from said board of aldermen.

Penalty.

SECT. 9. Any person, whether owner, lessee, contractor, or agent, who shall violate any of the provisions of this ordinance, shall forfeit and pay for every such violation the sum of one hundred dollars.

CHAPTER XXIII.

FIREWORKS, GUNPOWDER, AND OTHER EXPLOSIVE SUBSTANCES.

See G. S., c. 88, § 48. Right of inspection. St. 1877, c. 216, § 9.

Fireworks.

SECT. 1. No person shall set fire to any fireworks in the city of Worcester (other than those mentioned in the forty-seventh section of the eighty-eighth chapter of the General Statutes) composed of gunpowder, fulminating powder, spirits of turpentine, gun-cotton, or other combustible matter; or shall throw any such lighted fireworks, or shall have any such fireworks in his possession with intent to sell, or to set fire to the same, or shall offer for sale, sell, or give away any such fireworks, without license of the mayor and aldermen first obtained therefor.

SECT. 2. No gunpowder shall be kept by any Gunpowder. person in any place in the city of Worcester, unless it shall be kept in tight casks or canisters; and no gunpowder, above the quantity of twenty-five pounds shall be kept or deposited in any shop, store or other building, within ten rods of any other building, or transported from place to place in said city.

SECT. 3. No gunpowder above the quantity of Gunpowder, over one pound shall be kept or deposited by any person one pound. in said city, unless the same is well secured in copper, tin, or brass canisters holding not exceeding five pounds each, closely covered with copper, tin or brass covers, according to the forty-eighth section of the eighty-eighth chapter of the General Statutes.

SECT. 4. No gun-cotton nor any substance pre- Explosives. pared for explosion shall be kept by any person within the limits of the city, excepting under the regulations and penalties that are now applicable by law to gunpowder.

CHAPTER XXIV.

FREE PUBLIC LIBRARY.

See St. 1860, c. 14, printed on page 84.

Ordinance
affirmed.

SECT. 1.   The first section of an ordinance passed on the twenty-third day of December, in the year eighteen hundred and fifty-nine, entitled an ordinance for the establishment and government of the " Free Public Library of the city of Worcester," is hereby re-ordained and affirmed.

Directors, eligibility and election of.

SECT. 2.   The members of the board of directors heretofore chosen shall continue to hold their offices for the term for which they were respectively chosen, and there shall be chosen in the month of December, annually, by ballot, by the city council in convention, two directors to fill the vacancies occurring on the first day of January next ensuing, which directors shall hold their office for the term of six years from the first day of said January; and all vacancies in said board occasioned by death, resignation, removal from the city or otherwise, shall be filled in like manner as they arise, for the unexpired term thereof; and no person shall be eligible to fill a vacancy arising from the expiration of his term of office.

SECT. 3. The directors shall meet as soon as Organization. may be after the first day of January of each year, and organize themselves into a board by the choice of president and secretary from their own number; and a majority of said board shall be required for the transaction of business.

SECT. 4. The secretary shall have the care and Secretary. custody of all books, records, papers, and documents belonging to the board, and shall record all the doings of said board in a book to be furnished by said city; and he shall deliver said books, records, papers and documents to his successor in office.

SECT. 5. The board of directors shall have full Librarian and subordinate power to appoint a librarian and all subordinate officers. officers whom they may deem expedient, fix their compensation, and remove said officers at pleasure.

SECT. 6. All moneys appropriated for the public Expenditures. library shall be expended by said board of directors for paying the librarian and his assistants, warming and lighting the building, furnishing it and keeping it in repair, in purchasing books, keeping the building and books insured, and for such other things as may in their judgment be for the benefit and advantage of the institution.

Directors,
powers of.

SECT. 7.   The said board of directors shall have the care and custody of the building and grounds so far as they may be used and occupied by the public library, shall have the sole custody of the books and management of the library, and shall have full power to make any and all needful and suitable regulations concerning said library and the use thereof.

Reports.

SECT. 8.   The said directors shall, annually, in the month of January, lay before the city council a detailed report of their doings, and of the condition of the library.

CHAPTER XXV.

HACKNEY AND OTHER CARRIAGES.

G. S. c. 19, § 14; 120 Mass., 60.

Licenses and
stands.

SECT. 1.   The mayor and aldermen may from time to time at their discretion grant licenses, upon such terms and to such persons as they may deem expedient, to set up, employ, or use hackney carriages for the conveyance of persons for hire, from place to place within the city of Worcester, and may designate the public stand or stands within said city which said carriages may occupy, and no person shall set up, employ, or use such carriage for the purpose aforesaid without a license therefor as aforesaid.

SECT. 2. Every person licensed according to the provisions of section one of this chapter shall give a bond with sufficient surety or sureties, to be approved by the city clerk, in such sum as the mayor and aldermen may order, conditioned for the safe conveyance of passengers and their baggage, according to the provisions of this chapter, or such rules and regulations as the mayor and aldermen may prescribe ; and no person shall behave himself in a rude and disorderly manner ; nor use any indecent, profane, or insulting language towards any person or persons, nor be guilty of being intoxicated.

Bonds and be-havior.

SECT. 3. Every person licensed as aforesaid shall cause his carriage to be conspicuously marked with the number assigned to it by the city clerk, in metallic figures, not less than one and a half inches in size, and of such color as to be readily seen and read ; and the names of the owners and driver and the number of the carriage, together with the rates of fare duly established, shall be conspicuously posted on a printed card in every such carriage. And no owner, or driver, or other person having charge of any hackney carriage, shall demand or

Carriages to be numbered.

Notice to be posted.

12

receive any more than the price or rate of fare
established by the board of aldermen, under a
penalty not exceeding twenty dollars and he shall
forfeit his license. And for unreasonably refusing
to carry any passenger from any railroad station to
any point within the city, the owner, driver, or
other person having charge of such hackney carriage, shall be subject to a like penalty.

SECT. 4. No license granted as aforesaid shall
apply to any carriage, or owner, or driver, except
the particular one designated therein by its number
or otherwise made certain.

SECT. 5. No owner, driver, or other person having charge of any hackney carriage shall stand or
wait for employment, with such carriage, in any
street, square, lane, court, or public place, within
said city, other than the stands assigned to such carriages by the mayor and aldermen or by some person
by them duly authorized.

SECT. 6. Every owner, driver, or other person
having charge of any hackney carriage which has a
stand in any street or square, or at any railroad
depot, or place of public entertainment, shall at all
times when driving or waiting for employment wear
a badge on his hat or cap, with the number of his
carriage thereon, in brass or plated figures of not

less than one-half inch in size, and so placed that the same may be distinctly seen and read.

SECT. 7. Every hack, stage coach, omnibus, or Definition. other vehicle, whether on wheels or runners, which shall be used for the conveyance of passengers for hire from place to place within said city shall be deemed a hackney carriage within the meaning of this chapter.

SECT. 8. The mayor and aldermen may from Job wagons, &c. time to time grant licenses, to such persons and upon such terms as they may deem expedient, to employ or use any wagon, cart, sleigh, or other vehicle, which may be necessary for the conveyance from place to place within said city, for hire, of any goods, wares, furniture, merchandise or rubbish; and the mayor and aldermen may designate the public stand or stands within said city which such vehicles may occupy, and no person shall use any of the vehicles mentioned in this section for the purpose herein specified without a license as aforesaid.

SECT. 9. For every license granted under the Fees for licenses. provisions of this ordinance there shall be paid to the city clerk the sum of one dollar for the use of the city.

Expiration and transfer.

SECT. 10. All licenses granted as aforesaid shall expire on the first day of May next after the date thereof, and no license shall be sold, assigned or transferred without the consent of the mayor and aldermen indorsed thereon by the city clerk or his assistant and the payment of one dollar.

Job wagons, &c. To be numbered, &c.

SECT. 11. Every person licensed under the provisions of section eight of this ordinance shall have placed upon the outside and upon each side of the vehicle he may use the name of the owner and the number of the license, in plain legible words and figures of not less than one and one-half inches in size, and so that the same may be distinctly seen.

Position at stands.

SECT. 12. All drivers, owners, or persons having the care of any such carriages or vehicles as are described in this chapter, while at the stands designated by the mayor and aldermen, shall place their respective carriages or vehicles next to the sidewalk, in a single line, and so as to leave sufficient space for travellers along the streets and passageways, and so as not to obstruct or encumber the crossing places of any street.

Minors.

SECT. 13. No hackney carriage or other vehicle mentioned in this chapter shall be driven by a minor unless he be specially licensed by the mayor and aldermen.

SECT. 14. The mayor and aldermen may establish Fare.
the fare for the conveyance of passengers in any
hackney carriage licensed according to the provisions of this chapter, and revise or change the same
at pleasure.

SECT. 15. No owner, driver, or other person Excessive fare.
having charge of any hackney carriage for the
conveyance of passengers, licensed as aforesaid,
shall demand or receive a higher rate of fare than
that established by the mayor and aldermen.

SECT. 16. Whoever wantonly violates any of Penalty.
the provisions of this chapter shall have his license
forthwith revoked, and he shall not again be
licensed for the term of three months thereafter;
and this penalty shall be in addition to any other
penalty imposed or provided by virtue of this ordinance for the violation of the provisions aforesaid.

CHAPTER XXVI.

HEALTH.

See St. 1877, c. 133 (accepted). G. S., c. 26.

SECT. 1. The board of health shall consist of Constitution and
three persons, one of whom shall be the city organization.
City physician,
physician *ex-officio*, and shall meet on the first St. 1878, c. 21.

Monday of February, annually, or as soon as practicable thereafter, and organize by the choice of one of their number as chairman ; they may choose a clerk, who may or may not be a member of the board, and may make such rules and regulations for their own government, and for the government of all subordinate officers in their department, as they may deem expedient.

Clerk.

Regulations.

Powers.

G. St. c. 26, §§ 4, 5, 6.

SECT. 2.   Said board of health are hereby authorized to prepare and enforce such regulations as they may deem necessary for the safety and health of the people, with reference to house drainage and its connection with public sewers, where such connection is made, and shall have power to appoint such subordinate officers, agents and assistants, as they may deem necessary, and may fix their compensation, and the compensation of the clerk before mentioned ; *provided*, that the whole amount of such compensation shall not exceed the sum appropriated therefor by the city council.

Reports.

St. 1877, c. 133, § 4 (accepted).

SECT. 3.   Said board of health shall, annually, in the month of January, present to the city council a report made up to and including the thirty-first day of the preceding December, containing a full and comprehensive statement of the acts of the board during the year, and a review of the sanitary condition of the city; they shall also, whenever the city council or the committee on finance shall so require, send to the auditor an estimate in detail of the appropriations required by their department during the next financial year.

SECT. 4. Whenever the board of health shall be satisfied that any building used as a dwelling house is not furnished with a sufficient drain, privy and vault, or water closet, or either of them, they shall give notice in writing to the owner of such building, or his agent, or such notice may be left at the last and usual place of abode of such owner, agent or occupant, requiring that a suitable drain, privy and vault, or water closet, or either of them, be constructed within such time as they shall appoint, for the use of such tenement; and in case such requisition be not complied with the board shall cause such drain, privy and vault, or water closet, or either of them, to be constructed, the expense of which shall be charged to such owner or agent; *provided* that notice to persons residing out of the state, or to unknown owners of such buildings, the premises being unoccupied, may be given by posting up the same on the premises, and by advertising in some newspaper published in the city of Worcester.

May enforce regulations.
St. 1877, c. 133, § 5 (accepted).
G. S., c. 26.

May abate nui-
sances.
G. St. c. 26, §§ 7,
8, 9, 10. SECT. 5. Whenever it shall appear to the board of health that any cellar, lot or vacant land is a nuisance, or in such condition that it may probably become dangerous to the public health, they shall cause the same to be drained, filled up, or otherwise prevented from becoming or remaining a cause of nuisance or sickness; and shall charge all reasonable expenses incurred in so doing to the owners or parties occupying such cellar, lot, or land; *provided* that notice shall have been first given, and forty-eight hours thereafter allowed, as provided in the fourth section of this chapter.

Prosecute offend-
ers and remove
nuisances.
G. St. c. 26, § 11. SECT. 6. The board of health shall cause all persons who persistently violate or disobey the laws of the commonwealth, or the rules of the board of health, or the orders, by-laws, or ordinances of the city for the preservation of the health of the city, which are now in force, or which shall hereafter be made by lawful authority, to be forthwith prosecuted and punished; and in case, in the opinion of the board of health, it shall be for the health or comfort of the inhabitants that any particular nuisance shall be forthwith removed, and without delay, it shall be their duty to cause the same to be removed accordingly at the expense of the owner or owners of the land upon which the said nuisance exists.

SECT. 7. Whenever the board of health shall find that the number of persons occupying any tenement is so great as to be the cause of nuisance or sickness, or a source of filth; or whenever any tenement is not furnished with a suitable privy, vault, and drain under ground according to the provisions of this chapter, the board of health may cause all or any persons occupying such tenement to be removed therefrom, first giving them notice in writing to remove, and allowing them at least forty-eight hours in which to comply with said notice.

Crowded and filthy tenements.

SECT. 8. The board of health shall have power to remove, or cause to be removed, from any dwelling house or other place within said city, any person or persons sick with any contagious or infectious disease, or any person who may have been exposed to such contagious or infectious disease, to any hospital or place within the city proper for the reception of such sick or exposed person; and, in case any person sick with such contagious or infectious disease in any house or other place within said city cannot be removed without danger to his or her health, the board of health shall have power to cause any house or tenement contiguous to be vacated by the removal of the occupants thereof, for such time as said

Contagious and infectious diseases.

G. St. c. 26, §§ 16, 17.

board shall think expedient, and as the safety of
the inhabitants may require.

Swill, &c.
St. 1874, c. 225.

SECT. 9. The mayor and aldermen may license
suitable persons to collect and carry away, through
the public streets and highways of the city, swill,
house offal, and decayed or decaying vegetable or
animal matter.

Swine and goats.

SECT. 10. The mayor and aldermen are authorized to prohibit the keeping of swine and goats in
any part or parts of the city, where they deem that
the keeping of such animals would be detrimental
to the health or comfort of the citizens in the neigh-
borhood thereof residing or passing, and shall have
power to remove or cause to be removed any swine
or goats from any place where the keeping of such
animals is prohibited.

CHAPTER XXVII.

LAMPS.

Lamps and
fixtures.

SECT. 1. The committee on lighting streets shall
have the care and oversight of all the street lamps
and fixtures belonging to the city; shall cause the
same to be kept clean and in good order for use, and

shall see that the same are kept lighted at such times as the convenience of the public requires. They shall also cause such other lamps to be lighted as the city council may from time to time direct. Lighting lamps.

SECT. 2. The said committee may employ suita- ble persons to light and extinguish the street lamps, may contract for materials, and shall see that the posts, lamps and fixtures ordered and located by the city council are procured and erected. Lighting and extinguishing lamps. Contracts for fixtures, &c.

CHAPTER XXVIII.

MESSENGER.

SECT. 1. The city messenger shall have the gen- eral care and custody of the city hall building and its various apartments, together with the steam heat- ing apparatus. He shall attend the sessions of the city council, school committee, and board of over- seers of the poor, and deliver all messages, notifica- tions, and other papers, when thereto directed by the mayor, the president of the common council, the city council, or either branch thereof; and shall no- tify the members of all committees of the city coun- cil, joint or separate, of any meeting of the same, when requested by the chairman. He shall prepare Messenger. Duties of.

and arrange the halls and apartments of the city hall
building for the uses to which they may be appropriated; and, under the direction of the mayor, he
shall provide all things necessary and proper for the
use of said halls and apartments, shall keep them
clean and in good condition for ordinary uses, and
for any occupation which shall be permitted by the
mayor and aldermen, or common council, shall personally attend to, prepare and take charge of any of
said halls and apartments, whenever the occupation
of them shall be permitted as aforesaid; and shall
be at all times subject to such further orders as the
city council or either branch thereof may make.

CHAPTER XXIX.

MILK INSPECTOR.

Inspector.
Duties of.

SECT. 1.   It shall be the duty of the inspector of
milk to cause the provisions of chapter two hundred
and nine of the acts of the year 1880 to be published
once in some newspaper published in the city of
Worcester, to obtain evidence and prosecute all
violators of the laws relating to the sale of milk, and
to publish the names of all persons convicted of
violating said laws in at least two newspapers
printed in said city, and also to grant licenses to
persons dealing in milk in the city, as provided in
said chapter.

CHAPTER XXX.

OVERSEERS OF THE POOR.

SECT. 1. The overseers of the poor shall elect a Clerk to be elected. clerk who may or may not be one of their own number. He shall be sworn to the faithful performance of the duties of his office, and shall keep a fair and intelligible record of all the doings of the overseers of the poor, and of all facts relating to any aid or assistance granted or refused by said overseers, and, at the expiration of his term of office the record aforesaid shall be delivered to his successor in said office, or to the city clerk for the use of the city. He shall be governed in the Duties of. performance of his duties by such rules and regulations as may be prescribed by said overseers, or by any order or orders passed from time to time by the city council.

SECT. 2. It shall be the duty of said clerk to To keep accounts and prepare returns. keep an accurate account of all moneys received and expended by him, on account of the poor, and to make out and prepare for the overseers of the poor the annual returns and statistics required by law to be made to the secretary of the commonwealth.

SECT. 3. Said overseers shall cause books to be
kept, wherein shall be entered all information
required by the general laws of this commonwealth,
in regard to such persons as shall have been aided;
and also all further information in regard to every
case of relief given, or refused, that may be of
importance to the city of Worcester or the Commonwealth to preserve, stating the amount and
kind of aid given, and the reasons for giving such
aid, or for refusing the same; such information to
be so arranged as to be readily referred to upon
the books.

SECT. 4. All books, records, reports, papers and
property, belonging to said overseers may at any
time be examined by the board of aldermen, or any
person or committee which said board of aldermen
or the city council shall direct or appoint to inspect
and examine the same.

SECT. 5. Said overseers shall meet on the first
Friday evening of each month for the transaction
of the general business of the board, and at such
other times as they may from time to time order or
direct at any regular meeting, or at any time when
called to meet by order of the mayor.

SECT. 6. During the month of December in each
year said overseers shall submit to the city council a

full report of all their doings, receipts and expenditures for the year ending with the last day of the November preceding, together with such information and suggestions as they shall deem it expedient to present to the city council, or shall be requested to furnish by an order of the board of aldermen or city council; and they shall, whenever requested by the board of aldermen or city council, communicate such information as may be desired by either.

CHAPTER XXXI.

PAWNBROKERS AND DEALERS IN SECOND-HAND ARTICLES.

SECT. 1.   No person shall carry on the business Pawnbrokers,&c. to be licensed. of a pawnbroker or keeper of a shop for the purchase, sale or barter of junk, old metals or second-hand articles, in the city of Worcester, unless he is G. s, c. 88, § 28. duly licensed therefor by the mayor and aldermen.

SECT. 2.   Every pawnbroker or keeper of such a To keep books, shop shall keep a book, in which shall be written at the time of receiving any article as a pawn, or purchasing any article, a description of the same, the name, age and residence of the person from whom, and the day and hour when he received or purchased it, and such book shall at all times be open to the inspection of the mayor and aldermen and of any person by them authorized to make such inspection.

Not to receive of minors.

SECT. 3. No person licensed as aforesaid shall, directly or indirectly, receive any article in pawn or purchase any article of any minor or apprentice, knowing or having reasonable cause to believe him

St. 1877, c. 185.

to be such. All articles received in pawn or purchased may be examined by the mayor and aldermen, or by any person authorized by them

Examination.
1876, c. 147.

to make such examination, at all times. All licenses granted under this ordinance shall designate the place where the person licensed may carry on his business, and he shall not engage in or carry on his business in any other place than the one

Licenses.
For regulations, see St. 1879, c. 102.

designated ; and all the provisions of this ordinance shall be incorporated into every license which shall be granted under it.

CHAPTER XXXII.

MANUFACTURE, STORAGE AND SALE OF CAMPHENE, AND PETROLEUM AND ITS PRODUCTS.

Licenses.
G. S., c. 88, § 51.
St. 1869, c. 152, § 9.

SECT. 1. Any person desiring to manufacture, refine, mix, store or keep for sale, in the city of Worcester, camphene, burning fluid or other explosive or inflammable fluid, or any oil or fluid composed wholly or in part of any of the products of petroleum except as provided in the fifth section of chapter one hundred and fifty-two, of the acts of the year eighteen hundred and sixty-nine, shall make application in writing for a license therefor to the board of aldermen of said city, and shall state in such application the locality, building or part of a building, for which he desires a license, and whether he desires a license for manufacturing, refining, and mixing said articles, or any of them, or a license for storing or keeping them, or both.

SECT. 2. No license shall be granted for selling, or keeping for sale, for illuminating purposes, any kerosene or refined petroleum which has not been inspected by the officers appointed for that purpose by the mayor and aldermen.

Inspection. St. 1869, c. 345.

SECT. 3. Except as herein before expressly provided, licenses may be granted for manufacturing, refining, mixing, storing and keeping said articles, or any of them, in cellars, or upon the first floor of buildings, or in other suitable localities, in such quantities and in such a manner as the board of aldermen may in each case determine, except that no license shall be granted for manufacturing, refining, mixing, storing or keeping said articles, or

Licenses, limitation of. St. 1869, c. 152, §§ 6, 9.

14

any of them, upon the first floor of any building in a greater quantity than thirty gallons, unless the same be contained in metallic vessels, securely closed.

Conditions and revocations of licenses. St. 1869, c. 152, § 9.

SECT. 4. There shall be expressed in said license the name of the person or persons to whom the license is granted, and such conditions, and limitations as to the manner in which said articles shall be mixed or kept, as the board of aldermen may in each case see fit to impose. All persons holding such license shall allow the chief engineer of the fire department, or any of the assistant engineers, or the inspector or inspectors appointed by the mayor and aldermen, to enter the premises described in the license, and take such samples of oils and make such examinations of the premises as said engineers or inspectors deem expedient; and the board of aldermen may revoke any license at any time.

Violations of licenses.. St. 1869, c. 152, § 6.

SECT. 5. It shall be the duty of the chief and assistant engineers of the fire department, and of the inspectors appointed by the mayor and aldermen, to make complaint to any court of competent jurisdiction of all violations of the provisions of chapter one hundred and fifty-two, and chapter three hundred and forty-five, of the acts of the year eighteen hundred and sixty-nine, and to bring suits in the name of the mayor of the city against all persons who manufacture, refine, mix, store or keep for sale camphene, burning fluid or other explosive or inflammable fluid, or any oil or fluid composed wholly or in part of the products of petroleum, without the license required by this ordinance.

CHAPTER XXXIII.

PHYSICIAN.

SECT. I. The city physician shall hold office for the term of three years from the first Monday of February next succeeding his appointment, and shall be *ex-officio* a member of the board of health. He shall, in addition to his duties as a member of said board, attend, under the general direction of the overseers of the poor, upon all sick paupers and patients under the care of the city authorities at the poor farm or elsewhere within the limits of the city, and render all services incumbent upon him by any law of the state or ordinances of the city. He shall report annually on the second 'Monday of January, to the city council, a list of all persons who have died while under his charge during the previous year, stating the age, sex and disease of the person

Physician.
Term of office.
Duties of.

deceased : shall give to either branch of the city council or to any committee thereof, all such professional advice and counsel as they may require of him; shall vaccinate all scholars of the public schools who may be sent to him by the school committee for that purpose, free of charge, and perform all such professional services as may be reasonably required of him by the mayor, aldermen, city council or board of health.

Duties of.

SECT. 2.   He shall perform all the professional services that may be required in the police station ; shall keep a record of all cases of small-pox or other contagious diseases and make such reports thereof as the mayor and aldermen may from time to time direct.

CHAPTER XXXIV.

POLICE.

Charter, § 13.

Department, of what composed.

SECT. 1.   The police department of the city of Worcester shall consist of one city marshal, two assistant marshals, one captain of night police, and such number of policemen as the mayor and aldermen may from time to time appoint.

Marshal to give bond.

SECT. 2.   The city marshal, before entering upon the duties of his office, shall give bond in the sum of one thousand dollars, with sufficient sureties, to be approved by the mayor and aldermen, for the faithful performance of the duties of said office.

SECT. 3. The city marshal shall have the general Duties. charge and supervision of all the constables, assistant marshals, and police officers, shall have the precedence and control of the same whenever engaged in the same service, and shall report forthwith to the mayor and aldermen any violation of duty on the part of either of said officers. It shall be his duty from time to time to pass through the streets, lanes, alleys, squares and public grounds of the city, to observe all nuisances, obstructions and impediments therein, or on the sidewalks thereof, and cause the same to be removed according to law. He shall receive all complaints against any person or persons for any breach of the laws, or of the ordinances of the city, and for that purpose shall attend, at his office, daily, at some stated time to be designated by the mayor and aldermen. He shall report immediately to the commissioner of highways any defect he may discover in any of the streets, roads, or bridges. He shall prosecute all offenders with promptness and effect, and use all lawful and proper means to secure convictions. It shall be his duty to enforce and carry into effect all laws and city ordinances, and to be vigilant to detect and punish any breach thereof. He shall obey and execute all orders of the mayor and aldermen, the city council, or of the board of health.

Duties with regard to public health.

SECT. 4. It shall be the duty of the city marshal, subject always to the direction, authority and control of the board of health, to carry into execution all the ordinances and rules made by the city council and all rules made by the board of health relative to causes of sickness, nuisances and sources of filth that may be injurious to health, or may affect the comfort of the inhabitants of the city, existing within the limits thereof; to report all such nuisances, sources of filth, and causes of sickness to the board of health; and to cause all such nuisances, sources of filth and causes of sickness to be removed, destroyed or prevented, when practicable, as the case may require, conformably to such ordinances and rules, and the laws of the commonwealth.

Duties about nuisances, &c.

SECT. 5. The city marshal, when thereto ordered by the board of health, shall, at any time between sunrise and sunset, enter into any building or other place in the city, for the purpose of examining into, destroying, removing or preventing any nuisance, source of filth, or cause of sickness therein; and in case such entrance is opposed he shall make known such opposition to the board of health, in order that a warrant may be obtained to enforce the same as provided by law.

SECT. 6. The city marshal shall keep or cause to be kept, at the police station, a complete descriptive list of each and every person arrested and brought to the station, by giving his or her name, nativity, age, height, complexion, weight, color of hair and eyes, the amount of money he may have in his possession, his present residence, and the offence for which he is arrested, all of which shall be entered in a book to be furnished by the city; and the same shall be delivered by said marshal to his successor in office.

To keep records at station.

SECT. 7. The city marshal shall keep a correct record of all the doings of his office, which shall at all times be subject to the inspection of the mayor and aldermen, and shall make a regular report thereof as often as once in three months to the city council, and at such other times as they shall require.

To keep records of doings.

SECT. 8. The assistant marshals before entering upon the duties of their office shall give bond in the sum of five hundred dollars, with sufficient sureties, to be approved by the mayor and

Assistant marshals to give bonds.

aldermen, for the faithful performance of the duties of their office.

General duties of. SECT. 9. The assistant marshals shall, under the direction of the marshal or of the mayor and aldermen, aid in any and all such duties as are prescribed in this chapter for the city marshal, and may act as day and evening police.

Duties at fires. SECT. 10. The assistant marshals shall, in case of fire in the city, repair to the place where the fire may be, and attend diligently to the preservation of the public peace, the prevention of thefts, and the loss or destruction of property.

Special police. SECT. 11. The mayor and aldermen may appoint such number of special police, for day or night service, as they may deem necessary, and fix their compensation.

Water, duties of officers about. SECT. 12. It shall be the duty of each and every police officer to exercise supervision over the use of water, to prevent its waste, and to report to the office of the water commissioner all cases of leaks in water pipes which may come to their knowledge, and the locations where any waste is permitted by takers; and for this purpose they shall have free access at all times to any premises, apartments or rooms

where they have good reason to believe water is being improperly used or wasted.

SECT. 13. The city marshal may establish rules Rules and regu-
and regulations for the government of the police, lations.
subject to the approval of the mayor and aldermen.

SECT. 14. All fees, penalties, and witness fees Fees.
received in the Central District Court of Worcester St. 1862, c. 216, § 15.
by any police officer receiving a stated salary, and
all compensation for any service performed by them
in their official capacity, shall be paid by such officer
into the city treasury.

CHAPTER XXXV.

POUND KEEPERS.

SECT. 1. Every pound-keeper in the city of Wor- Pound keeper to keep record.
cester shall keep a record of all his doings, together
with a list of all animals by him impounded, with
the names of the owners thereof, which record shall
be at all times open to the inspection of the mayor
and aldermen or of any person by them authorized
to make such inspection.

15

CHAPTER XXXVI.

PUBLIC GROUNDS.

Charter, § 21.

Taking horses on public grounds.

SECT. 1. No person shall ride, lead, or drive any horse in or upon any inclosed public grounds in the city of Worcester, except by the permission of the commissioners of public grounds and shade trees.

Injuring fences around.

SECT. 2. No person shall injure or deface any fence around any public grounds in said city.

Creating nuisance on and digging, &c., gravel, &c.

SECT. 3. No person shall, in any manner, carry or cause to be carried into any of the inclosed public grounds in said city any dead carcass, filth, or any offensive matter or substance whatever, nor dig or carry away any of the sward, gravel, sand, turf or earth in or from said grounds, except by permission of the commissioners thereof; and no person shall commit any nuisance on any of said inclosed public grounds.

Trespass by animals.

SECT. 4. No person shall suffer any horse, ox, cow, grazing animal, or fowl belonging to him, or under his care or keeping, to go at large on any public grounds in said city.

SECT. 5. No person shall lie upon any seat or Lying on seats or ground, or playing games. upon the ground upon the Central park or common, or Elm park, or play at any game on said parks or commons, except upon such parts thereof as may be designated by the commissioners of public grounds and shade trees.

CHAPTER XXXVII.

SCHOOLS.

SECT. 1. The school committee may appoint and Superintendent, election, compensation and duties of. fix the compensation of a superintendent of public schools, a majority vote of the whole board being St. 1874, c. 272. necessary for that purpose. Said superintendent shall have the care and supervision of all the public schools of the city, under the direction and control of said school committee, and shall hold his office until a successor is appointed or he is removed; and he shall be removable at the pleasure of the school committee.

SECT. 2. The school committee shall present to Committee to furnish estimates. the auditor on or before the twentieth day of December in each year an estimate of the amount required for salaries, for incidental expenses, and for the alteration, repairs, and erection of school-

houses for the year commencing with the first day
of said December.

SECT. 3. Said committee shall be the original
judges of the expediency and necessity of having
additional or improved accommodations for any
public school within the limits of the city ; and
whenever, in their opinion, a school-house is
required, or material alterations are needed, they
shall send a communication to the city council,
stating the locality and the nature of the further
provisions for schools which are wanted; and no
school-house shall be located, or materially altered
until the school commitee shall have approved of
the proposed locality and plans.

School accommo-dations.
St. 1873, c. 183, printed on page 35.

SECT. 4. The school committee may cause any
scholar of any of the public schools within said city
to be vaccinated by the city physician ; and no
person who has not been vaccinated, or otherwise
secured against contagion of small pox, shall be
permitted to attend any of the public schools within
the city of Worcester. It shall be the duty of the
school committee to carry the provisions of this
section into effect, and for that purpose to make
any necessary rules and regulations.

Vaccination.
G. S., c. 41, § 9.

CHAPTER XXXVIII.

SEAL.

SEC. 1. The seal of the City of Worcester shall Seal. be of circular form, having in its centre the figure of a heart, encircled with a wreath, and in the margin the words " Worcester a Town, June 14, 1722 ; a City, February 29, 1848."

CHAPTER XXXIX.

SEALER OF WEIGHTS AND MEASURES.

SECT. 1. It shall be the duty of the sealer of Sealer to publish notices. weights and measures to annually give public St. 1876, c. 123, notice, by advertisements to be published each day $ 1.   St. 1877, c. 151. for one week, in one or more of the daily papers of the city, to all persons having a usual place of business in the city who use scales, weights or measures, for the purpose of selling any goods, wares, merchandise or other commodities, or for public weighing, to bring in their scales, weights, and measures, to be adjusted and sealed; and said sealer shall attend, at one or more convenient places, to be designated in said notice, and shall adjust, seal and record all scales, weights and measures so brought in.

Duties.
St. 1876, c. 123,
§ 2. St, 1877,
c. 151.

SECT. 2.   At any time after said notice the sealer shall go to the houses, stores and shops of persons mentioned in section one, who have neglected to comply with the said notice, and, having entered the same, with the assent of the occupant thereof, shall adjust and seal their scales, weights and measures; and shall collect for said service the

Compensation.

compensation set forth in section fourteen of chapter fifty-one of the General Statutes, and pay the same to the city treasurer, on or before the thirtieth day of November in each year, reporting at the time of payment the amount thereof to the auditor.

Duties and sal-
ary.
St. 1876, c. 123,
§ 8.

SECT. 3.   The said sealer shall perform all the other duties prescribed in chapter one hundred and twenty-three of the Statutes of 1876, and any statute in amendment thereof, and shall receive a salary, to be fixed by the city council, annually.

CHAPTER XL.

SEWERS.

See St. 1867, c. 106, printed on page 68.   St. 1871, c. 354, printed on page 72.

Superintendent
to have charge,
&c.

SECT. I.   The superintendent of sewers shall, under the direction of the committee on sewers,

have charge of the repair and construction of the
sewers and drains of the city.

SECT. 2. The city council of the city of Worces- City council to
ter shall cause to be constructed and kept in repair
all main drains and common sewers which shall be
ordered to be laid down through any streets or
private lands within said city.

SECT. 3. All common sewers shall be laid, as Sewers to be in
centre of streets.
nearly as practicable, in the centre of the streets
through which they pass, and no person shall enter
his particular drain into any common sewer or drain Permission to
enter.
without a permit in writing from the superintendent
of sewers.

SECT. 4. He shall grant permits to individuals Permission to
enter.
to enter their drains into the public sewers and
drains, in accordance with the rules and regulations
made therefor by the city council, and shall keep
a complete record, in books made for that purpose,
of such permits, giving the name of the street, and
the number of the estate, if any, name of the
owner, size and kind of side drain entered, and Record.
the name of the drain layer making the entrance,
and such other facts in connection therewith as
may be of importance as matter of record.

Drain layers.   SECT. 5. No person as a drain layer shall make any entrance into any sewer in the city unless he be duly licensed by the mayor and aldermen; and such person so licensed shall give a bond, in a sum of not less than one thousand dollars, for the faithful performance of such work as he may execute, and to make good any defects which may appear in any sewer, street, pavement or drain, in consequence of any work done under any permits granted him, or which may appear in the work so done by him.

Obstructing sew-   SECT. 6. No person shall throw any earth, dirt,
ers, &c.   stones, bricks, sawdust, ashes, cinders, shavings, hair, oyster, lobster or clam shells, or any animal or vegetable substance, into any drain or sewer, inlet, man hole or catch basin, in the city of Worcester.

Particular drains.   SECT. 7. All particular drains which shall here-after enter into any common sewer shall be built of such materials, dimensions, and descriptions, with such grade and in such manner as the city council shall direct; and they shall be at all times subject to be enlarged or otherwise altered by the city council, as in their judgment the public health
Superintendent   or convenience shall require. The superintendent
to keep accounts
and report.   shall keep an accurate account of the expense of

constructing and repairing each common sewer, and shall report the same to the joint standing committee on sewers, together with a schedule of property belonging to the department; and said committee shall, on or before the first Monday of January in each year, present to the city council a report containing a statement of the condition of all the sewers of the city, and of the property con- nected therewith, with an account in gross of all expenditures for the year ending November thirtieth next preceding, together with any suggestions and information which they may deem important.

Committee on sewers to report.

CHAPTER XLI.

SIDEWALKS.

See St. 1869, c. 390, printed on page 76.

SECT. 1. Whenever the city council shall adjudge that the public convenience and necessity requires that a sidewalk be laid out and established in the city of Worcester, the order for laying out and establishing the same, with a written description of the boundaries, admeasurements, grades and heights of the curbstone thereof, shall be filed in the office of the city engineer, and shall remain on file seven days, at least, before the passage by either board of the order laying out and establishing said sidewalk.

City council to lay out side- walks.

16

Commissioner to build, &c.

SECT. 2. When any sidewalk shall have been laid out and established as aforesaid, the commissioner of highways, under the direction of the committee on highways and sidewalks, shall grade the same, set the curbstone, pave the gutters, and construct said sidewalk of such material as the city council shall deem expedient. It shall be the duty of said commissioner to keep an exact account of all expenses and outlays required or incurred by him in constructing each sidewalk, abutting upon any estate, and report the same in writing within thirty days from the completion of the same, with the names of persons chargeable with the whole or any part of such expense, to the auditor, who shall at once report the same to the city council, and they shall forthwith proceed to assess upon the owners of the several estates abutting upon said sidewalks their just and proportionate part of the expense of paving said walk. Said report shall contain in separate items the expense of paving the gutters, setting the curbstone and paving the walk.

To keep accounts and report.

City council to assess abutters.

What shall be assessed.

SECT. 3. The expense of constructing or repairing any sidewalk laid out and established as aforesaid, or any sidewalk heretofore established in the city of Worcester, shall be assessed upon the abutters, but no part of the expense of grading the street, setting the curbstone or paving the gutters shall be so assessed, but shall be paid for by the city.

SECT. 4. Whenever the public convenience and safety requires that any sidewalk heretofore established in the city of Worcester be repaired, the city council shall order the commissioner of highways, under the direction of the committee on highways and sidewalks, to repair the same, and he shall forthwith cause the same to be repaired, and report the expense of so doing to the auditor in the same manner as is provided in section two; and the auditor shall report the cost of the same to the city council, and it shall be assessed as provided in section two.

Repairs.

SECT. 5. The city council may cause temporary footpaths or walks to be graded or constructed at the expense of the city, in front of vacant lots or elsewhere, where the public convenience or interest does not require that permanent sidewalks shall be laid out and established as herein before provided; and such temporary walks shall be subject to all the restrictions and regulations contained in this chapter.

Temporary footwalks.

CHAPTER XLII.

SINKING FUNDS.

St. 1875, c. 209.

Commissioners, election and duties of.

SECT. 1.   There shall be elected by a concurrent vote of both branches of the city council a board of commissioners of the sinking funds, consisting of three persons, one of whom shall be elected each year, in the month of December, and shall hold office for the term of three years, from the first Monday of January next following said election ; said board shall have the sole care and management of any and all sinking funds established in con-

Incompatability. City Treas., St. 1875, c. 209, § 5.

formity to law.   No member of the city council shall be a member of said board.   In case of a

Vacancies.

vacancy the remaining member or members shall exercise the powers of the board till the vacancy shall be filled.

Organization.

SECT. 2.   Said commissioners shall meet on the first Monday of January, annually, or as soon as practicable thereafter, and organize by the choice of a chairman, secretary and treasurer.

Treasurer.

SECT. 3.   The treasurer may be the city treasurer, and, if the city treasurer shall be chosen, his bond shall apply to and include duties performed under this ordinance.   If any other person shall be

chosen as treasurer, he shall give a·bond, with sureties, to the satisfaction of the commissioners, for the
proper performance of the duties of his office. The Commissioners to
keep a record
commissioners shall keep a record of their proceed- and report.
ings ; and, annually, in the month of January, make
a written report to the city council of the amount
and condition of the funds under their management,
and the income thereof, for the then preceding
financial year. The record and the securities be- Record and securities.
longing to said funds shall at all times be open to
the inspection of the mayor and aldermen, or of any
committee of the city council duly authorized for the
purpose. The treasurer shall receive such compen- Compensation.
sation as shall be fixed by the city council, but no
commissioner shall receive compensation for his
services.

SECT. 4. It shall be the duty of the commission- Commissioners to
report the sums
ers aforesaid, on the third Monday of December in required.
each year, to report to the auditor the amount
required to be raised by taxation at the next annual
assessment for each of the sinking funds in the
hands of said board for the redemption of the city
debt; and, to ascertain the amount to be so raised
by taxation, they shall deduct from the total amount
of the required annual contribution thereto all additions to such funds during the year preceding said
third Monday of December from the several sources

of income specified in section eight of this ordinance.

To invest. It shall further be the duty of said commissioners, so far as they may be able, to invest, from year to year, any contribution to the several sinking funds, in bonds of the funded loans of the city, and to hold the same as part of the sinking fund to which any such contribution shall be made under section five of chapter two hundred and nine of the Acts of 1875;

To stamp bonds. and the commissioners shall cause to be written or stamped on the face of said bonds, a notice that they are a part of said sinking fund and are not negotiable, and the coupons thereof as they become due and are paid shall be cancelled.

Application of funds. SECT. 5. The commissioners aforesaid shall in no case pay or apply any sinking funds or the interest or accumulation thereof in payment of interest

Renewal. upon any debt of the city. Upon the maturity of the funded debts of the city outstanding December 20, 1875, the same shall be renewed in securities of the city, payable on or before the first day of June, A. D. 1905, except so far as the same or any portion thereof may be paid at maturity, or may be provided for by the funds in the hands of the commissioners.

When payable. SECT. 6. Any debt contracted by the city under section three of chapter two hundred and nine of the Acts of 1875, shall be payable within a period

not exceeding ten years from the date of contracting the same, *provided, however*, that debts incurred
in constructing general sewers shall be payable
within a period not exceeding twenty years from
the date of contracting the same, and debts incurred
in supplying the inhabitants with pure water shall
be payable within a period not exceeding thirty
years from the date of contracting the same.
Whenever any debt is contracted as aforesaid, City to establish
and as provided in this section, the city shall, at when debt is
the time of contracting the same, establish a sinking fund, and shall contribute thereto from year to
year an amount annually raised by taxation sufficient with its accumulations to extinguish the debt
at maturity, and every such sinking fund shall
remain sacred and inviolate, pledged to the payment
and redemption of said debt, and shall be used for
no other purpose, and the commissioners aforesaid
shall receive all sums contributed thereto and
invest and apply the same as provided in section
five of chapter two hundred and nine of the Acts
of 1875.

SECT. 7.   Whenever any debt to be paid from any Payment.
sinking fund becomes due, the commissioners shall
apply from the funds in their care, applicable thereto, so much of said funds, or the proceeds thereof,
as may be necessary for the payment of said debt,

and any excess of said funds after the payment of said debt shall be applied to the sinking fund for the extinguishment of the general debt of the city, and all scrip, notes and bonds of the city, when paid by the commissioners, shall be cancelled by them and delivered to the city auditor.

Certain funds to be added to sinking funds.

SECT. 8. All sums of money which may be received on account of the sale of real estate of any description, now belonging, or which may hereafter belong to the city, excepting such as may be held for the benefit of the city hospital; all sums which may be received on account of the principal sum of any bond or note now owned, or which may hereafter be owned by the city, excepting such as may be held for the benefit of said hospital; all sums which may be received on account of assessments for any benefit and advantage by the laying out, altering, widening, grading or discontinuing of any street, or on account of assessments for the construction of drains and sewers; all excess of income from water rates over the amount required for maintenance and repair of the water works and interest on the funded water debt, and all excess of appropriations over the amounts required for the purpose thereof, shall, at the close of the financial year, be added to any sinking fund or funds which the city council may designate; and, if the city council shall

City council to designate.

fail to designate to which of said sinking fund or funds the several sums above mentioned shall be applied, the commissioners of the sinking funds may apportion and apply the same in such manner as shall reduce the amount to be raised by taxation for said funds.

CHAPTER XLIII.

SOLICITOR.

SECT. I. It shall be the duty of the city solicitor to draft all bonds, deeds, leases, obligations, conveyances and other legal instruments, and do every professional act which may be required of him by the city council, the mayor, or by any committee or ordinance of the city council, or by any order or rule of the city council, or either branch thereof; also, when required by the mayor and aldermen, common council, or any committee of the city council, or of either branch thereof, he shall furnish a written opinion on any legal question or subject which may be submitted to him ; and he shall at all times furnish legal advice to any officer of the city who may require his opinion upon any subject concerning the duties incumbent upon such officer by virtue of his office. He shall also attend all meetings of the city council or either branch thereof ; and, when requested, he

City solicitor, duties of.

17

shall attend the meetings of any committee of the city council.

Duties of.   SECT. 2.   He shall commence and prosecute all suits brought by order of the city or on account of any estate, claim, rights, privileges or demands of the city; and shall appear before any court in this commonwealth in defence of all actions or suits against the city or its officers in their official capacity, wherein the rights, estates, privileges, ordinances, or acts of the city, or breach of any ordinance may be called in question; also shall try and argue any and all causes in which the city shall be a party, before any tribunal, whether in law or equity, in this commonwealth, or before any referee, arbitrator, or board of commissioners.

To report and deliver papers, &c., to his successor.   SECT. 3.   He shall, annually, in the month of January, make a report to the city council of the business of his office during the preceding year, stating the suits pending in favor of or against the city at the time said report is made, with a brief description of each; and he shall deliver to his successor in office all papers, records of suits, documents or other information he may have; relative to any claim for or against the city.

CHAPTER XLIV. .

STABLES.

G. S. c. 88, § 32.

SECT. 1.   No person shall erect, occupy, or use Stables for over four horses. any building for a stable for more than four horses in the city of Worcester, except in such part thereof as the mayor and aldermen shall direct.

SECT. 2.   No building shall be erected within the Livery stables. city of Worcester, and used and improved as a stable for keeping horses or carriages, upon hire or to let, commonly called livery stables, within one hundred feet of any church or meeting-house erected for public worship, without the consent in writing of the proprietors of such church or meeting-house, or the religious society or parish worshipping therein, and the consent of the mayor and aldermen.

CHAPTER XLV.

STANDS FOR HAY, STRAW, WOOD, BARK AND CHARCOAL, AND
DUTIES OF WEIGHERS AND MEASURERS THEREOF.

For bark see Charter, § 31 ; G. S., c. 49, §§ 184, 186.　For hay see G. S., c. 49, §§ 72 to 83 (§§ 72 to 75 have been accepted, and §§ 76 and 77 are repealed).　For coal see Charter § 31, St., 1870, c. 205.　For lumber, &c., see charter, § 31, G. S., c. 49, § 184.　For straw see St., 1861, c. 67.

Stands for hay, &c.
Charter, § 31.
G. S., c. 49, §§ 72, 73 (which have been accepted).

Public scales.

SECT. 1.　The mayor and aldermen shall appoint a suitable place or places in the streets and squares of the city of Worcester, as a stand or stands for the measurement, weight, and sale of hay, straw, wood, bark and charcoal ; and the city council shall from time to time, as the public good may require, establish a sufficient number of public scales, furnished with decimal weights, for the weighing of hay and other articles.

Sellers to stand only at designated places.
Charter, § 31.
G. S., c. 49, §§ 72, 73.

SECT. 2.　No person driving or having charge of any vehicle containing hay, straw, wood or charcoal for sale, shall stand with such material for more than ten minutes in any public street, square or place in said city, other than such stand or stands as shall be designated by the mayor and aldermen.

Certificates.
Charter § 31.
G. S., c. 49, §§ 72, 73.

SECT. 3.　All certificates or tickets that may be issued by any weigher of hay or straw, or any measurer of wood, bark, or charcoal, shall express the quantity or weight thereof measured or weighed in words at length, and not in figures only, and the same shall be written or printed with ink, and not in pencil marks.

SECT. 4.   No weigher of hay or straw, or measurer To weigh, &c., of wood, bark or charcoal, shall give or permit to be personally. G. S., c. 49, § 73, given a ticket of any measurement or weight not (accepted). made by himself in person.

SECT. 5.   The weighers of hay or straw, shall Weighers to make return to the auditor, before the tenth day of make returns and pay over, one every month, of all fees received by them by virtue half their fees. G. S , c. 49, § 73. of their said office, during the month preceding, and shall, within ten days after said return, pay over one-half of said fees to the city treasurer as provided by law.

SECT. 6.   Every measurer of wood, bark or char- Measurers to coal, in said city, shall keep a record of all the keep record. G. S., c. 49, § 73. tickets issued by him, with the date thereof, the names and places of residence of the respective drivers, and the quantity of each load, which record shall at all times be subject to the inspection of the mayor and aldermen ; and at the expiration of his term of office it shall be delivered to the city clerk.

Measured wood only, to be offered for sale, &c.
Charter, § 31.
G. S., c. 49, §§ 72, 73.

SECT. 7. No person shall bring into said city for sale, nor shall offer for sale or sell in said city, any wood, hay, straw, bark, or charcoal by the measurement or weight of any person other than some public measurer or weigher, duly appointed.

Weighers, duties of.
G. S., c. 49, § 72.

SECT. 8. It shall be the duty of every weigher to attend to the scales that may be assigned to him, to deliver to the driver or owner of every load of hay, straw or other article weighed, a certificate specifying the name of the driver or owner, his place of residence, the article or merchandise weighed, the weight and tare, the fees charged and received, and the date and number of the certificate. He shall keep a record, in a book to be furnished by the city, of all hay and other articles weighed by him, and shall deliver said book to the city clerk at the expiration of his term of office. Said record shall contain all the particulars that are required to be stated in the certificate aforesaid.

Certain sales forbidden.

SECT. 9. No owner or driver of any wagon, cart, sled or other carriage containing hay, straw, bituminous or mineral coal, for sale in larger quantities than five hundred pounds, shall proceed to deliver the same within the city, without first causing the same to be weighed by some of the weighers appointed by the mayor and aldermen.

CHAPTER XLVI.

STREETS — LAYING OUT.

See Charter, § 28. Betterment law, St. 1871, c. 382; St. 1874, c. 275.
Cannot use certain parks and lands of state, St, 1875, c. 163.

SECT. 1. No street, highway or town way shall be laid out, altered, or discontinued in the city of Worcester, except upon petition therefor, and unless, seven days, at least, previous thereto, the board of aldermen shall cause written notice of their intention to lay out, alter or discontinue the same, to be left at the last and usual place of abode of the owners of the land over or through which such way is proposed to be laid out, altered or discontinued, or unless such notice shall be delivered to such owner in person, or to his tenant or authorized agent; *provided* that if the owner shall have no known place of abode in the city, and no tenant or agent therein known to the mayor and aldermen, then such notice shall be posted up in some public place in the city seven days at least before laying out, altering or discontinuing of such way. Said notice shall specify the time and place appointed by the board of aldermen for meeting and hearing the parties interested therein.

SECT. 2. At the time and place appointed and

Mayor and alder- notified as aforesaid, the board of aldermen shall
men, duties of.
meet, and hear all persons or parties interested
claiming to be heard, and proceed to view the premises; and the mayor and aldermen may thereupon,
if they shall see fit, and shall adjudge that the public convenience and necessity requires it to be done,
proceed to lay out, alter, widen or discontinue said
street or highway, and shall determine what damages, if any, are sustained by any persons in their
property, by the laying out, altering, or discontinuing of such way or road, and the amount of compensation they shall severally receive; and said mayor
and aldermen shall fix the boundaries and admeasurements of said proposed street or way, and shall
report their action in the premises to the common
council.

Not to be laid   SECT. 3.   No street, town way, or private way,
out, &c., until,
&c.   which may be laid out, altered, or discontinued by
the mayor and aldermen, shall be established, until
such laying out, alteration or discontinuance, with
the boundaries and admeasurements of said way, and
also the amount of damages which said mayor and
aldermen shall determine has been sustained by any
persons in their property, by such laying out, alteration, or discontinuance, shall have been reported to
the common council, and accepted and allowed at a
regular meeting thereof, nor unless the decree or

order for laying out, altering, or discontinuing such street or way, shall have been filed in the office of the city clerk, seven days at least before such meeting of the common council.

SECT. 4. No street or town way shall hereafter be Width and grade. opened in the city of less width than forty feet, except with the consent of the mayor and aldermen in writing first had and obtained, for that purpose, and no person shall open a private street into Private streets. any public street of the city until the grade of such private street shall have been fixed and established by the city council, the expense of fixing the grade to be paid by the party applying to open the street, and the city council reserving the right to close the same when unsafe or inconvenient for travellers.

SECT. 5. Whenever any street or highway shall Stone monuments. be laid out and established as a highway in the city of Worcester, it shall be the duty of the commissioner of highways, under the direction of the committee on highways and sidewalks, to cause to be placed at all the angles thereof good and substantial stone monuments, with a hole of suitable size and depth drilled near the center of the uppermost end. In all cases where circumstances may require that the monument shall be sunk even with the

18

surface of the ground or pavement, the distance from the hole in said monument to one or more permanent objects in the immediate proximity of the same shall, if practicable, be ascertained and consti-- tute a part of the record of the laying out of said street.

CHAPTER XLVII.

STREETS.

See Charter, § 35. G. S., c. 18, § 11.

Names.   SECT. 1. The several streets in the city of Worcester shall continue to be called and known by the names by which they are now called and known until the same shall be altered by the city council; and the city council may change or alter the name of any street, highway or public place; and said council shall establish the names of all streets, highways, and public places hereafter laid out and accepted by said city, or by any other authority, within said city.

Obstructions.   SECT. 2. No person shall break or dig up the ground in any highway or street, or erect thereon any staging for building, or place thereon any building material, or any goods, wares, or merchandise, or any coal, dirt, rubbish, or obstruction of any kind, or occupy any portion of a highway or street for the purpose of erecting, repairing or moving any building, without a written license from the mayor and aldermen; and any person licensed as aforesaid who shall break or dig up the ground, pavement or sidewalk, shall, before the expiration of the license, restore the same to the acceptance of the commissioner of highways.

Moving buildings, &c.

SECT. 3. In all cases in which a license may be given for obstructing or excavating any highway or street, the board of aldermen may impose such conditions and limitations as they shall see fit with regard to erecting barricades, maintaining lights, and taking other precautions for the security of travellers and other persons. Such license shall also express the time for which it shall continue in force.

Conditions of license.

SECT. 4. Every person receiving such license shall execute a written agreement to indemnify and save harmless the city against all damage or cost by reason of any claim for damages, or any process, civil or criminal, on account of the existence of such obstruction or excavation, or any injury to any person occasioned thereby; and the mayor and aldermen may, in their discretion, require sureties for the performance of such agreement.

Licensee to give bond.

204   ORDINANCES.

Temporary obstructions.

SECT. 5. The foregoing prohibitions shall not prevent the unloading or temporary deposit in the street or sidewalk of merchandise, fuel, building materials, or other articles in course of carriage to or from premises adjacent or neighboring, provided that such articles shall be removed forthwith on request of the commissioner of highways and shall in no case be suffered to remain more than six hours.

Posts.

SECT. 6. No person shall erect or remove any post or posts in any street or public place in said city except by permission of the mayor and aldermen.

Injuring trees, &c., in streets or on public lands. G. St., c. 46, § 7.

SECT. 7. No person shall dig up, injure or destroy any ornamental or shade tree, shrub, or vine, growing and being in any of the streets or highways, or on any of the public lands of said city, without the consent of the commissioners of public grounds and shade trees first obtained therefor in writing.

Blasting.

SECT. 8. No person shall blast any rock or other substance with gunpowder, or other explosive material, at any place within fifty rods of any street or public place in said city, without a license from the mayor and aldermen in writing specifying the terms and conditions on which such license is granted.

SECT. 9.   No person shall ring, or cause to be _{Ringing bells,} rung any bell, or use or cause to be used any horn _{&c., in streets. St. 1875, c. 136.} or other instrument, in any street in said city, to give notice of any business or calling, or for the sale of any article.

SECT. 10.   No person shall stand in any street in _{Standing in streets to sell articles, &c.} said city for the purpose of grinding cutlery, or for the sale of any article, or for the exercise of any other business or calling.

SECT. 11.   No person shall water any of the _{Watering carts.} streets, lanes, alleys, courts, or public places in said city, by or with a watering cart, without first having obtained a license therefor from the mayor and aldermen.

SECT. 12.   No person shall post up any placard, _{Posting bills, &c. St. 1873, c. 349.} handbill, poster or notice upon any building, tree, tree-guard, box, fence or any other thing, without the consent of the owner, agent or occupant, nor _{Bulletin boards.} shall any person erect and maintain bulletin-boards in any street, highway or public place in said city, without a license from the mayor and aldermen.

SECT. 13.   No person shall course, coast, or slide _{Coasting. St. 1875, c. 136.} down, across, in, or along any of the streets or high-ways of said city, upon any hand-sled board, or otherwise, except in such places and under such restrictions as the mayor and aldermen shall designate and require.

Fencing, &c., adjoining streets, &c.

SECT. 14. No person shall erect or cause to be erected any fence or building adjoining any street or public ground in said city, without having first ascertained the bounds of the same by application to the city engineer.

Obstructing sidewalks.
St. 1875, c. 136.

SECT. 15. No person shall drive any horse, cart, or wheel carriage, or wheel, push, or draw any wheel-barrow or hand-cart, or other vehicle, or suffer or allow any ox, horse, cattle, cart, wheel carriage or wheel-barrow to be on the sidewalk of any street or highway of said city, except for the purpose of crossing as near as may be at right angles to such sidewalk, and in order to go into or out of some adjoining enclosure; *provided* that this section shall not apply to children's carriages drawn

Driving over hose.

by hand; nor shall any person drive any carriage or other vehicle upon or over any hose pipe, or hose, in use at any fire, placed in any street or highway by order of the chief engineer or other officer of the fire department.

Fast driving.
St. 1865, c. 31.
St. 1867, c. 20.

SECT. 16. No person shall ride in any carriage or drive any horse or horses in any highway or

street in said city at a rate of speed exceeding eight
miles per hour; nor in such manner as to endanger
or unreasonably incommode passengers therein.

SECT. 17. No person shall stop with any team or *Obstructing streets with teams.*
carriage across any highway or street in said city in
such a manner as to hinder or obstruct the travel *St. 1875, c. 136 St. 1876, c. 20.*
over said highway or street, nor at the side of or so
near to another team as to obstruct public travel in
any highway or street in said city.

SECT. 18. No person shall stop with any team *Obstructing cross walks.*
or carriage, or place any obstruction of any kind, *St. 1875, c. 136. St. 1876, c. 20*
upon any flag or stepping stones, or other footwalk,
across any street or highway in said city.

SECT. 19. No owner or person having the care *Pasturing, &c., animals.*
of any swine, sheep, goats, horses, mules, or neat *G. S., c. 45, § 10.*
cattle, shall permit or suffer the same to go at large,
or to pasture in any street, sidewalk, highway, common, square, or other public place, or remain upon
any sidewalk within said city.

SECT. 20. No person shall suffer any horse, ox, *To be fastened.*
mule, or team of any kind, owned by him or under *St. 1876, c. 20.*
his charge, to remain standing without being
securely tied or fastened, or to go at large without
a rider or driver, in any street, highway, or public
place in said city.

Not to be fasten-
ed to lamp posts,
&c.
SECT. 21.   No person shall tie or fasten any horse, ox, mule, or team of any kind, to any lamp post, or to any ornamental or shade tree, shrub, or vine, or to any fence or other thing erected for the protection of such tree, shrub, or vine, in any street, highway, or public place in said city.

Fences, porticos,
&c.
G. S., c. 19, § 13.
117 Mass., 114.

Hoisting.
SECT. 22.   No person shall erect, set up or maintain any fence, portico, platform, or doorstep extending into any highway, street, or sidewalk, in said city, and no person shall hoist any material from any street into a building adjoining the same so that said material while being hoisted shall overhang any part of said street, after notice from the city marshal that the apparatus used for that purpose, or the manner of doing the same, is in his opinion unsafe until said party shall have obtained apparatus therefor, and until he shall do the same in a manner satisfactory to the city marshal.

Signs and awn-
ings.
SECT. 23.   No person shall establish or maintain any wooden or metallic shade or awning, sign, signboard, or inscription of any kind, before his or her place of business, or dwelling house in said city, over any part of said public street or sidewalk, unless the same be safely and securely supported, so as to in no wise incommode travellers, and so that the lowest part of said sign, sign-board, inscription or shade,

shall be at least eight feet in height above the street
or sidewalk ; and no person shall establish or maintain over any part of any public street or sidewalk
any other awning or shade, unless the lowest part
of the same shall be at least seven feet above the
said street or sidewalk, and unless the same shall be
securely fastened to the building to which they may
be affixed ; *provided*, however, the mayor and aldermen may order any sign, sign-board, awning or
shade, which may project over any part of said street
or sidewalk, to be removed at any time when they
may so determine.

SECT. 24. No person shall place or cause to be Merchandise.
placed, or suspend or cause to be suspended, in front
of any building, or place of business, on or over any
sidewalk, highway, or street in said city, any goods,
wares, merchandise, or any other thing, so that the
same shall project or extend more than three feet
over said street or sidewalk without permission of
the mayor and aldermen ; or where the same shall
unreasonably incommode travellers.

SECT. 25. No person shall suffer his fire-wood, Fuel.
coal, or other fuel, in any quantity, to remain unnec- G. St., c. 45, § 8.
essarily on any sidewalk, or in any street, lane, alley
or public place in said city over night, or after
twilight in the evening ; and in case it must of

19

necessity remain the said owner shall cause a sufficient light to be placed and kept over and near the same throughout the whole night.

Sawing wood.
G. St., c. 45, § 8.

SECT. 26. No person shall saw any wood or pile the same on any sidewalk of any street or highway of said city, and no person shall stand on any such sidewalk with his wood-saw or saw-horse to the hindrance or obstruction of travel over the same.

Cellar doors.
St. 1867, c. 241.

SECT. 27. No person shall suffer a cellar door, or cellar doorway, from any sidewalk or street in said city, into any cellar or basement, to be kept open when not in immediate use; nor when in immediate use, after the beginning of twilight, unless a good and sufficient light be constantly kept at the entrance of such door or doorway.

Cellars, &c., un-
covered.
St. 1867, c. 241.

SECT. 28. No cellar, vault, cistern, or well shall be kept uncovered, in or near any street or public place in said city, unless the same be enclosed by a safe and sufficient fence, curb or guard.

Games.

SECT. 29. No person shall, within the limits of any street or highway in said city, play at any game of ball or foot ball, throw any snow-ball, stones or other hard substance, drive or roll a hoop, fly any kite, or engage in any other amusement, game or

exercise, interfering with the free, safe, and convenient use of such street or highway by any persons
travelling or passing along the same ; nor shall any Gaming.
person promote or encourage the fighting of birds
or animals in any street, highway, or public place in
said city.

SECT. 30.   No person shall swim or bathe, unless Bathing.
properly clothed, in any of the waters within the
city, so as to be exposed to the view of spectators
from any building, highway, street, or railroad.

SECT. 31.   No person shall allow any sink water, Sink water, &c.
or other impure water, to run from the house, barn
or lot occupied by him, or under his legal control,
into any street or highway in said city.

SECT. 32.   No person shall allow any gate, or Gates, &c.
door, belonging to premises owned or occupied St. 1867, c. 241.
by him, or under his legal control, and adjoining
any sidewalk, street, or highway in said city, to
swing on, over, or into said sidewalk, street or
highway.

SECT. 33.   No person shall wantonly mar, injure, Injuring fences, &c.
deface, or destroy any fence, guide-post, sign-board,
awning, lamp post, lamp or lantern in any street,
highway, or public place in said city; and no

Extinguishing lamps. person shall light or extinguish any public lamp in any street or highway in said city, except by permission of the committee on lighting streets.

Removing snow.
G. St., c. 45, § 9. SECT. 34. The tenant, occupant, and in case there shall be no tenant or occupant, the owner, agent, or person having care of any building or lot of land bordering on any highway, street, lane, court, square, or public place within said city where there is any footway or sidewalk duly established, shall cause all the snow to be removed from such footway or sidewalk, so far as the same shall abut on said building or lot of land.

When to be re-moved.
G. St., c. 45, § 9. SECT. 35. If the snow shall cease to fall on any day before six o'clock in the forenoon it shall be removed as provided in section thirty-four before twelve o'clock noon of the same day, and if the snow shall cease to fall after six o'clock in the forenoon of any day and before four o'clock in the afternoon of the same day, it shall be removed as provided in said section within four hours after it ceases to fall; and if the snow ceases to fall after six o'clock in the afternoon of any day and before twelve o'clock in the afternoon of said day, it shall be removed as provided in said section before ten o'clock in the forenoon of the day next succeeding; and this section shall apply to snow which may have fallen

from any building abutting on said sidewalk or footway.

SECT. 36. Whenever any sidewalk, or foot-way, ^{Ice.} or any part thereof, mentioned in section thirty-four, ^{G. St., c. 45, § 9.} abutting on any building, or lot of land, shall be encumbered with ice, the occupant, or the owners, agent or person having charge of such building or lot, shall cause such sidewalk or footway to be made safe and convenient for travel, so far as it abuts upon said lot of land or building, by removing the ice therefrom, or by covering the same with sand or some other suitable substance.

SECT. 37. The tenant, occupant, and in case ^{Roofs, snow and ice on.} there shall be no tenant, the owner, agent, or person ^{St. 1863, c. 86.} having the care of any building adjoining any highway, street, lane, court, square, or public place within said city, where the roof of said building slopes towards said highway, street, lane, court, square, or public place, shall cause all the snow and ice to be removed from such roof. If the snow shall fall or the ice form in the day or night time, it shall be removed from such roof within twenty-four hours after the same shall have ceased falling or forming.

SECT. 38. No person owning or having the con- ^{Discharging water on sidewalks.} trol of a building upon land adjoining a street through which a common sewer is laid shall suffer any water from the roof, gutters, conductors, or water spouts of such building to be discharged, or to flow over or upon any street or sidewalk.

Discharging water on sidewalks.

SECT. 39. Every person owning or having the control of a building upon land adjoining a street through which a common sewer is laid shall cause all water from the roof, gutters, conductors, and water spouts of such building to be conducted by suitable pipes, properly laid, into the common sewer; or shall cause the roof, gutters, conductors and water spouts of such building to be so constructed and arranged that no water shall or may be discharged or flow therefrom over or upon any street or sidewalk.

Penalty.

SECT. 40. Whoever is guilty of any violation of sections thirty-eight and thirty-nine, of this ordinance, shall forfeit and pay to the use of said city the sum of twenty dollars; and shall further be liable for all damages sustained by the city or by any person injured, through the accumulation of ice upon any street or sidewalk, or otherwise, by reason of such violation.

Behavior in streets, near buildings, on door-steps, &c.

SECT. 41. No person shall behave himself in a rude and disorderly manner, or use any indecent, profane, or insulting language in any street, highway, lane, alley, or other public place in said city or near any dwelling-house or other building therein; or be or remain upon any sidewalk, or upon any doorstep, portico, or other projection from any such house or other building, nor in any church, meeting-house, public hall, theatre, or entrance thereto, to the annoyance or disturbance of any person ; nor Frightening horses. shall any person, by any noise, gesture, or other means, wantonly and designedly frighten or drive any horse, in any street, highway, or other public place in said city.

SECT. 42. Three or more persons shall not stand Obstructing foot-together, or near each other, in any street of said walks. city, in such a manner as to obstruct a free passage for passengers therein or over any foot or sidewalk.

SECT. 43. It shall be the duty of any constable, Duties of officers. police officer, or watchman of said city to order any persons offending against the provisions of the preceding section to move on, and, if said order is not forthwith obeyed, to arrest the persons so offending.

SECT. 44. Whenever the word "street" or Street, definition "streets" is mentioned in this chapter, it shall be of. understood as including alleys, lanes, courts, public squares, and public places; and it shall also be understood as including the sidewalks, unless otherwise expressed.

Sidewalks, defini- SECT. 45. The sidewalks, within the meaning of
tion of and
record.   this ordinance, shall be such parts of the highway,
whether public or private, as are within the curbstones thereof, in all places where curbstones are
set; and also such parts of such highways as have
been established as foot or sidewalks, in conformity
to the then existing by-laws of the town of Worcester, or by ordinance or order of the city of Worcester, and also such parts of any street or highway as
shall be established and determined as foot or sidewalks, by the city council; and such laying out and
determination shall be recorded in the book of city
·records.

CHAPTER XLVIII.

SUPERINTENDENT OF PUBLIC BUILDINGS.

See St. 1875, Ch. 232.

Superintendent   SECT. 1. The superintendent of public buildings,
of public build-
ings to give a   before entering upon the duties of his office, shall
bond.   give a bond, with sureties, to be approved by the
mayor and aldermen, that he will not, directly or
indirectly for himself or others, or by others in trust
for him, or on his account, have any interest or con-
cern in any contract or agreement for the erection,
alteration or repair of any building belonging to the
city, or in any purchase, sale, or lease made by the
city under and by virtue of this ordinance.

SECT. 2. He shall, under the direction of the Duties. committee on public buildings, have the care and superintendence of the school-houses and all other buildings belonging to the city, except when other provisions are made by the ordinances of the city, and shall keep himself acquainted with their condition. He shall employ competent mechanics, and shall himself superintend all repairs that may be ordered on said buildings or fixtures thereof; and in general he shall render such services as may be required of him, in relation to such buildings, by the city council, or any committee or board appointed by the city council. He shall prepare for meetings the rooms designated for ward rooms, and shall have them cleaned and put in good order after any meeting therein.

SECT. 3. The superintendent of public buildings To be clerk of committee, keep shall be clerk of the committee on public buildings. a record and report. He shall keep an accurate record of all buildings and appurtenances thereto belonging, owned by the city, and, in the month of January, in each year, shall present to the city council a report in relation to the same, showing their condition, and the nature in detail and amount of expenditures that shall have been made in relation thereto, for the year ending with the last day of the November preceding.

20

To keep ac-
counts.

SECT. 4. Whenever the superintendent of public buildings shall sell any articles or materials belonging to the city, or shall do, or cause to be done, any work for any person or corporation, from which money shall become due to the city, he shall enter in books to be kept for that purpose, all such sales and work done, with the price thereof, and shall forthwith make out bills for the same and deliver them to the city auditor.

To be inspector
of buildings, and
duties as such.

SECT. 5 The superintendent of public buildings shall also be inspector of buildings as provided in chapter forty-seven of the Statutes of 1878, and shall perform all the duties prescribed for inspector of buildings in said Statute or any Statute which may be passed in amendment thereof. It shall be his duty to inspect all buildings more than two stories in height which may hereafter be erected in said city, and if in his opinion any building in said city used for public assemblies, for hotels, for lodging houses for the accommodation of more than twenty lodgers, or for manufacturing or work shops is not provided with proper facilities for escape in case of fire he shall immediately serve notice upon the owner, agent or other party having an interest in said building requiring such facilities to be provided without delay; and if the owner or person having charge of said building fails to furnish said facilities

for fourteen. days after service of said notice upon
him, he shall forfeit a sum of not exceeding one
hundred dollars.

CHAPTER XLIX.

TREASURER.

See Charter, § 19.

SECT. 1.   The treasurer of the city of Worcester Treasurer to be collector.
shall be collector of taxes.   He shall be sworn to To be sworn and give bond.
the faithful performance of his duties as treasurer
and collector, and give a bond to said city, with
sufficient sureties, to the satisfaction of the mayor
and aldermen, in such sum as they may prescribe,
that he will faithfully perform the duties of his office,
and justly and truly account for and pay over all
moneys in his hands belonging to said city.

SECT. 2.   The treasurer shall, under the direction To keep accounts and report.
of the committee on finance, keep an accurate ac-
count of all his receipts and payments for and on
behalf of the city, making the same to conform, as
nearly as may be, with the accounts kept by the
auditor.   He shall, on the first Monday of January,
annually, make a report to the city council of all
such receipts and payments for the past financial Financial year.
year; and said financial year shall begin on the

first day of December, and end on the thirtieth day
of November in each year.

Duties of. SECT. 3. The treasurer shall have the custody of
all bonds given to said city by any or all officers
thereof, except his own, which shall be kept by the
auditor. He shall cause all books, papers and documents under his care belonging to said city to be
deposited and kept in a fire-proof vault or safe
belonging to said city, and shall deliver to his successor all books, papers, documents and property
belonging to said office. He shall make up his
annual account to the end of the financial year, and
render such service, and furnish such information
respecting the accounts and finances of said city, as
either branch of the city council, or any committee
Office hours. thereof, may from time to time require. His office
shall be kept open for business during such hours of
the day as the mayor and aldermen may determine.

To negotiate loans. SECT. 4. He shall, under the direction of the
committee on finance, negotiate all loans that may
be authorized by the city council; and whenever
any loan shall have been so authorized, and certificates of indebtedness ordered given therefor, said
certificates shall be signed by the mayor, the treasurer, and the auditor, and shall be registered in the
offices of said treasurer and auditor.

SECT. 5. It shall be the duty of the treasurer to Collection of collect and receive all rents or assessments which rents, &c. may be due said city, and all accounts and other demands against persons indebted to said city; and the receipt of the treasurer shall be deemed the only sufficient and valid discharge of debts due to said city; *provided, however,* that the superintendent of the almshouse, under the direction of the over- seers of the poor, may receive payment for articles sold from the poor farm, and shall account therefor with said overseers, and said articles shall be partic- ularly stated in the account rendered by said over- seers of the poor to the city council; *provided, also,* that the commissioner of highways may receive payments for articles sold by him, when the amount of such sale shall not exceed ten dollars, and may give receipts therefor; and the city marshal may receive payments for any extra police service author- ized by the mayor and aldermen, and his receipt therefor shall be valid.

SECT. 6. The collector, after receiving from the Taxes. assessors their tax list, shall, on or before the fifteenth day of September, in each year, proceed to collect the same as follows: To all persons who Discount. shall voluntarily pay their taxes on or before the tenth day of October next succeeding he shall allow a discount or abatement of six per centum, after which time no discount shall be made or allowed. On the fifteenth day of October, or as soon as practicable thereafter, he shall issue his

Costs.

summonses to those whose taxes are then unpaid, and in case said taxes be not paid on or before the

5 Allen, 563.

thirty-first day of said month, together with twenty cents for each summons, he shall then proceed to collect the same according to law; and he shall give notice by advertising and posting so much of this chapter as relates to the payment of taxes.

CHAPTER L.

TRUANT CHILDREN.

See St., 1873, c. 262.

Truants defined.

SECT. 1. Any child between the ages of seven and fifteen years, who is an habitual truant, or is found wandering about in the streets or public places of the city of Worcester, having no lawful occupation or business, not attending school, and growing up in ignorance, shall, upon conviction thereof, be committed to the truant school in said city, for a term not exceeding two years.

Truant officers.

SECT. 2. Truant officers, duly appointed, are

authorized and empowered to take into custody any such child and place him in the school to which he shall have been assigned by authority of the school committee of said city of Worcester.

SECT. 3. A truant school is hereby established Truant school. at the almshouse in said city, and assigned and provided as the place of confinement, discipline and instruction of all persons committed thereto according to law.

WORCESTER, DEC. 6, 1880.

This ordinance is approved by me.

ADIN THAYER,

Judge of Probate Court.

CHAPTER LI.

UNDERTAKERS.

SECT. 1. It shall be the duty of funeral under- Undertakers, duties of. takers themselves, or by their agents, who shall be persons of discreet and sober character, to attend, manage and conduct all funerals in the city of Worcester, and to attend to the removal of the bodies of deceased persons.

To obtain cer-
tificates.

SECT. 2. No funeral undertaker shall bury, or cause to be buried, the body of any deceased person, without having first obtained a certificate, as provided in chapter one hundred and seventy-four

Bodies not to be
buried without
permission of
undertakers.

of the Acts of the year 1878. No person shall bury or inter, or cause to be buried or interred, the body of any deceased person, in any of the public burial places of the city, without having first obtained permission from one of the funeral undertakers; and it is hereby made their duty to grant the same; but said permission shall not be granted till a certificate has been obtained therefor as aforesaid.

Removal of
bodies.

SECT. 3. No remains of any deceased person shall be removed from any grave or tomb in the city without the permission of one of the funeral undertakers, which permission it shall be their duty to grant to the nearest relatives or friends of the deceased; *provided*, no sufficient cause shall appear for refusing such assent, and it shall be the duty of the undertaker to attend himself to all such removals, and to enter in his book of records all the particulars attending such removal.

CHAPTER LII.

WARRANTS FOR WARD MEETINGS.

SECT. 1. The form of warrants for calling meet- Form of warrant
for ward meet-
ings of the citizens of the several wards shall be as ings.
follows :

CITY OF WORCESTER.

To either of the constables of the city of Worcester, Greeting:

In the name of the commonwealth of Massachusetts, you are hereby required forthwith to notify and warn the inhabitants of ward No.——— qualified to vote ——— to meet in ——— on ——— the ——— day of ——— at ——— o'clock in the——— noon, then and there to ———.

The polls shall be opened at —— o'clock, ——. M., and shall be closed at —— o'clock, ——. M.

Registration will cease at ——— o'clock, ——. M., on ———, and after the close of such registration no name will be entered on the check-list except as provided by ——.

And you are directed to serve this warrant by posting up an attested copy thereof at the place appointed for ward meetings in said ward ten days at least before the time of said meeting.

Hereof fail not, and make due return of this warrant and of your doings thereon to the clerk of said

21

ward four days at least before the time of meeting as aforesaid.

Witness ————— mayor of the city of Worcester, this ——— day of ——— in the year of our Lord one thousand eight hundred and ———.

By order of the mayor and aldermen.

————City Clerk.

Service and return.

SECT. 2. Service of a warrant, for calling a meeting of the citizens of a ward, issued by the mayor and aldermen, shall be made by a constable of the city, by posting up an attested copy of such warrant at the place appointed for ward meetings in said ward, ten days at least before the time of said meeting; and such warrant shall be returned to the clerk of said ward four days at least before the time of meeting.

Warrant for meeting of inhabitants.

SECT. 3. The form of warrants for calling meetings of the inhabitants of the city of Worcester shall be as follows:

CITY OF WORCESTER.

To either of the constables of the city of Worcester, Greeting:

In the name of the Commonwealth of Massachusetts, you are required forthwith to notify and warn the inhabitants of the city of Worcester, qualified to vote ——— to meet in ——— on ——— the ———

day of ———— at ———— o'clock in the ———— noon, then and there to ————.

The polls shall be opened at —— o'clock ——. M., and shall be closed at —— o'clock ——. M.

Registration will cease at —— o'clock ——. M., on ————, and after the close of such registration no name will be entered on the check-list except as provided by ————.

And you are directed to serve this warrant by posting up an attested copy thereof at the place appointed for ward meetings in each ward in the said city, ten days at least before the time of said meeting.

Hereof fail not, and make due return of this warrant and of your doings thereon to the city clerk four days at least before the time of meeting as aforesaid.

Witness———— mayor of the city of Worcester, this —— day of —— in the year of our Lord, one thousand eight hundred and ————.

By order of the mayor and aldermen.

———— City Clerk.

SECT. 4. Service of a warrant for calling a meet- Service and return. ing of the inhabitants of the city, issued by the mayor and aldermen, shall be made by any constable of the city, by posting up an attested copy of such warrant at the place appointed for ward meetings in each ward of the city, ten days at least before the time of said meeting; and each warrant shall be returned to the city clerk four days at least before the time of meeting.

Opening and closing polls. SECT. 5. It shall be the duty of the mayor and aldermen to fix the time when the polls shall close as well as the time for opening thereof, in the election of all officers, and to insert the same in the warrant calling the meeting for such elections.

CHAPTER LIII.

WATER COMMITTEE, COMMISSIONER AND REGISTRAR.

See Charter, § 36. Statutes printed on pages.40 to 67. St. 1875, c. 105.

Water committee, duties. SECT. 1. The committee on water shall have the general charge and supervision of the city water works and of all the property of the city pertaining thereto, and shall exercise a general supervision and control over all the business of the water department, and over all its officers and agents. They shall, at least once every six months, and as much oftener as they shall deem expedient, personally examine and inspect all aqueducts, reservoirs, dams, shops and premises belonging to the department. They shall have charge of the making of all contracts, and of the purchase of all materials and supplies, which may be required in carrying on the operations of said department. They shall examine and approve all bills for expenditures in said department, before they shall be allowed by the auditor.

SECT. 2.   Said committee shall, on or before the To report. twentieth day of December, in each year, present to the city council a report containing a statement of the condition of all the water works of the city, and of the lands and other property connected therewith, with an account in gross of all receipts and expenditures, together with any suggestions and information which they may deem important, and, at the same time, they shall transmit to the city council the reports of the water commissioner, the water registrar, and the city engineer relating to the water works.

SECT. 3.   The water registrar shall act as clerk of Water registrar, duties of. the committee on water at their meetings; he shall assess the water rates according to the tariff established by the city council; and he shall keep such books and records, make such reports and perform such other service as said committee may desire.

SECT. 4.   The water registrar, under the direction May abate water rates. of the committee on water, may make abatements in the water rates in all proper cases.

SECT. 5. The water commissioner, under the direction of the committee on water, shall have charge and care of the repair shop and pipe yard, tools and materials belonging to the department, and all main pipes, hydrants, gates, fountains, watering troughs and reservoirs belonging to the works. He shall exercise a constant supervision over the use of water, and attend to the enforcement of all regulations thereto. He shall keep an account of all tools, pipes, materials and other property in the shop and yard, and shall immediately repair all leaks or breaks, from any cause, in any main pipe, hydrant, gate, fountain, or watering trough, or service attached to the works ; and when in the performance of these repairs it becomes necessary to shut off the water from any pipe, he shall duly notify all takers thus to be deprived of water, except in a case of emergency ; shall put in such service pipes, lay such main and other pipes, and set such meters as may from time to time be directed by the committee on water; shall repair all injuries to any street, sidewalk, sewer or other public property caused by the water works, and may employ such assistants and laborers as may be approved by the committee ; he shall be vigilant and watchful in protecting the works from all nuisance and injuries, and keep them in complete and free working order at all times ; and he shall give immediate notice at the office of the water registrar of any accidents which may occur to any main or other pipe. In making repairs and laying pipes in any street, whenever said street is rendered dangerous by the obstructions thus caused, he shall cause the place to be suitably fenced, lighted and guarded. He shall neither purchase nor sell any materials in his department, except with the consent of or by an order from the committee on water; he shall keep a daily record of the height of the water in the reservoirs of the city; he shall make returns once a week of all labor done and materials used during the previous week; and, annually, on or before the twentieth of December, report to the committee on water the daily height of the water in the reservoir, the amount of pipe laid, giving the name of the street, the length, the number of gates and hydrants in each, the number and nature of leaks repaired, the number of services put in and meters set, and a full and complete inventory of all tools and materials in his charge, with their appraised value.

SECT. 6. The annual reports named in the pre- Reports.
ceding sections shall be made up to and include the thirtieth day of the preceding November.

SECT. 7. No person shall permit or allow any Waste.
Illegal use.
waste of water, and no person shall supply St. 1875, c. 105.

another with water who is not entitled to use the same.

Repairs, etc.
St. 1877, c. 105.

SECT. 8. No person or party except an officer or agent authorized by the committee on water, shall at any time remove or repair any meter, or fixtures connected therewith, which has been set or used by the department.

Increasing use.
St. 1875. c. 105.

SECT. 9. No new fixtures shall be put in, or alterations made in old ones, by which the consumption of water is increased, without the consent

Duties of plumbers.

of the committee on water. All plumbers doing business in the city shall, on the first of every month, make full returns to the water registrar, of the character and description of all work done by them, connected with the water works, during the month preceding. Any failure to report when requested, or any intentional concealment of work done, shall subject the offender to a fine of twenty dollars for each offence.

Tapping mains, &c.
St. 1875, c. 105.

SECT. 10. No person shall tap any street main, service or other distributing pipe, without authority so to do from the committee on water.

Opening and obstructing hydrant, &c.
St. 1875, c. 105.

SECT. 11. No person, except a fireman in the legitimate discharge of his duties as a fireman of the city of Worcester, shall open any hydrant, gate or service stop, without the consent of the committee on water, and no person shall place any building material or other article or rubbish of any kind, so as to hinder the free access to and use of any hydrant, stop cock, gate or other fixture.

CHAPTER LIV.

GENERAL PROVISIONS.

SECT. 1. When no other provision is made by virtue of this ordinance, or any law of the commonwealth, the mayor and aldermen may grant all licenses, not otherwise herein provided for, upon such terms and under such restrictions as they may prescribe, and revoke the same at pleasure. Licenses, how granted.

SECT. 2. When no other provision is made by virtue of this ordinance, or any law of the commonwealth, the mayor and aldermen may establish the rates of fare and the fees to be charged by any and all persons licensed by said mayor and aldermen for any service they may perform by virtue of such license; and said mayor and aldermen may revise, change, alter, or amend said rates of fare or fees at any time when the same may be required. Rates of fare and fees.

Licenses, how
issued.

SECT. 3. All licenses granted by the city council, or either branch thereof, shall be issued by the city clerk, bear the city seal, and be signed by the mayor or by such other city officer as the mayor and aldermen may direct.

Licenses by officers and boards.

SECT. 4. Whenever in this, or in any ordinance hereafter passed, anything is prohibited to be done without the permission or license of any officer, officers or board, such officer, officers or board shall have the power to permit or license such thing to be done.

Assessments.

SECT. 5. When no other provision is made by virtue of this ordinance, or any law of the commonwealth, the mayor and aldermen shall levy and apportion any and all assessments ordered to be levied by the city council, or either branch thereof.

Oaths of office
and bonds.

SECT. 6. Every city officer of the city of Worcester, before entering upon the discharge of the duties of his office, shall be sworn to the faithful performance thereof, and shall give such bonds as the mayor and aldermen may from time to time require.

Officers and office
hours.

SECT. 7. The several officers of the city of Worcester shall occupy such apartments in the city hall building or elsewhere as the mayor and aldermen may designate, and their office hours shall be fixed by the mayor and aldermen.

SECT. 8. When any ordinance repealing a former Repeal of a re-
ordinance, clause or provision, shall be itself repealed, nance.
such repeal shall not be construed to revive such
former ordinance, clause or provision, unless it shall
be therein so expressly provided.

SECT. 9. Whoever violates any law or ordinance Violation of
of the city of Worcester shall, unless where different Charter, § 35.
provision is made by such law or ordinance, or by
the laws of the commonwealth, forfeit and pay to
the use of said city a sum not exceeding twenty
dollars.

SECT. 10. All by-laws and ordinances heretofore Repeal.
passed by the city council of the city of Worcester,
are hereby repealed, except an ordinance relating to
the boundaries of the several wards of the city
passed November 16, 1875, but such repeal shall
not affect any act done, any right accrued, accruing
or established, the tenure of office of any person
holding office at the time it takes effect, or any forfeiture or penalty heretofore incurred.

SECT. 11. All future ordinances shall be promul- Promulgation.
gated by at least two insertions in some newspaper
published in the city of Worcester, to be designated
by the mayor and aldermen, and shall take effect
immediately upon such promulgation unless otherwise therein prescribed.

Enactment.   SECT. 12. All the foregoing ordinances having
been codified, revised and printed under the direction of a joint special committee on the revision of
the ordinances, and having also been revised by the
city council, are hereby declared to be the ordinances of the city of Worcester, and shall have the force
thereof, and shall take effect on the thirtieth day of
December, in the year one thousand eight hundred
and eighty, and all the ordinances repealed by this
chapter shall remain in force till that time,

IN COMMON COUNCIL, ⎫
Dec. 6, 1880. ⎬

Passed to be ordained under a suspension of the rules.
OLIVER P. SHATTUCK, *President.*

IN BOARD OF ALDERMEN, ⎫
Dec. 6, 1880. ⎬

Passed to be ordained by general consent.
FRANK H. KELLEY, *Mayor.*

Approved December 6, 1880.
FRANK H. KELLEY, *Mayor.*

CHAPTER LV.

WARDS.

Be it ordained, &c., as follows :

SECT. 1. The present division of the city of Worcester into Wards is hereby revised, and a new division thereof into eight Wards is hereby made, in accordance with section 3 of the charter of the City of Worcester, approved April 30th, A. D. 1866, and the general laws of the Commonwealth of Massachusetts; the said Wards shall hereafter be known and constituted as follows, viz :

WARD NO. ONE.

Beginning at the centre of Main Street at a point ^{Boundary of Ward One.} opposite the centre of Walnut Street; thence to and by the centre of Walnut Street to Chestnut Street; thence to and by the centre of Chestnut Street to a point opposite the centre of William Street; thence to and by the centre of William Street and in a direct line crossing West Street to the centre of Agricultural Street; thence in a direct line to the junction of Cataract Street with the boundary line between Worcester and Holden; thence by the boundary line between Worcester and Holden to the main track of the Boston, Barre and Gardner

Railroad; thence by the main track of the Boston, Barre and Gardner Railroad to its intersection with the main track of the Worcester and Nashua Railroad at Barber's Crossing; thence by the main track of the Worcester and Nashua Railroad to a point opposite the centre of Lincoln Square; thence to and by the centre of Lincoln Square to the centre of Main Street; thence by the centre of Main Street to the point of beginning, and contains 1342 voters.

WARD NO. TWO.

Boundary of
Ward Two.

Beginning at the centre of Main Street at a point opposite the centre of Exchange Street; thence by the centre of Main Street and Lincoln Square to the main track of the Worcester and Nashua Railroad; thence by the main track of the Worcester and Nashua Railroad to its intersection with the main track of the Boston, Barre and Gardner Railroad at Barber's Crossing; thence by the main track of the Boston, Barre and Gardner Railroad to the boundary line between Worcester and Holden; thence by the boundary line between Worcester and Holden and Worcester and West Boylston to the north-east corner of the city; thence by the boundary line between Worcester and West Boylston and Worcester and Shrewsbury to a stone monument set in the ground at the northerly end of Quinsiga-

mond Pond, and at an angle in said boundary line ;
thence by the boundary line between Worcester and
Shrewsbury to Belmont Street; thence to and by
the centre of Belmont Street to a point opposite the
centre of Shrewsbury Street; thence to and by the
centre of Shrewsbury Street to a point opposite the
centre of East Central Street; thence to and by the
centre of East Central Street to Summer Street ;
thence to and by the centre of Summer Street to a
point opposite the centre of Exchange Street;
thence to and by the centre of Exchange Street to
the point of beginning, and contains 1315 voters.

WARD NO. THREE.

Beginning at the centre of Main Street at a point Boundary of
opposite the centre of Exchange Street; thence to Ward Three.
and by the centre of Exchange Street to Summer
Street; thence to and by the centre of Summer
Street to a point opposite the centre of East Central
Street; thence to and by the centre of East Central
Street to Shrewsbury Street; thence to and by the
centre of Shrewsbury Street to Belmont Street;
thence to and by the centre of Belmont Street to the
boundary line between Worcester and Shrewsbury;
thence by the boundary line between Worcester and
Shrewsbury, Worcester and Grafton and Worcester
and Millbury to the centre of Grafton Street ; thence

by the centre of Grafton Street to the main track of the Boston and Albany Railroad; thence by the main track of the Boston and Albany Railroad to Green Street; thence to and by the centre of Green Street and Trumbull Square to Park Street; thence to and by the centre of Park Street to Main Street; thence to and by the centre of Main Street to the point of beginning, and contains 1359 voters.

WARD NO. FOUR.

Boundary of
Ward Four.

Beginning at the centre of Green Street at the point where it intersects with the main track of the Boston and Albany Railroad; thence by the track of the Boston and Albany Railroad to Grafton Street; thence to and by the centre of Grafton Street to the boundary line between Worcester and Millbury; thence by the boundary line between Worcester and Millbury to the centre of Granite Street; thence by the centre of Granite Street to its junction with Winthrop Street; thence to and by the centre of Winthrop Street to Vernon Street; thence to and by the centre of Vernon Street to a point opposite the centre of Endicott Street; thence to and by the centre of Endicott Street to Millbury Street; thence to and by the centre of Millbury Street to Green Street; thence to and by the centre of Green Street to the point of beginning, and contains 1368 voters.

WARD NO. FIVE.

Beginning at the centre of Green Street at the point where it intersects with the main track of the Boston and Albany Railroad; thence by the centre of Green Street to Millbury Street; thence to and by the centre of Millbury Street to a point opposite the centre of Endicott Street; thence to and by the centre of Endicott Street to Vernon Street; thence to and by the centre of Vernon Street to a point opposite the centre of Winthrop Street; thence to and by the centre of Winthrop Street to Granite Street; thence to and by the centre of Granite Street to the boundary line between Worcester and Millbury; thence by the boundary line between Worcester and Millbury, and Worcester and Auburn to the main track of the Norwich and Worcester Railroad; thence by the main track of the Norwich and Worcester Railroad to the main track of the Boston and Albany Railroad near the Junction Depot; thence by the main track of the Boston and Albany Railroad to Southbridge Street; thence to and by the centre of Southbridge Street to a point opposite the centre of Madison Street; thence to and by the centre of Madison Street to a point opposite the centre of Portland Street; thence to and by the centre of Portland Street to Park Street; thence to and by the centre of Park Street and

23

Trumbull Square to Green Street; thence to and
by the centre of Green Street to the place of beginning, and contains 1374 voters.

WARD NO. SIX.

Beginning at the centre of Main Street at a point
opposite the centre of Park Street; thence to and
by the centre of Park Street to a point opposite the
centre of Portland Street; thence to and by the
centre of Portland Street to Madison Street; thence
to and by the centre of Madison Street to where it
intersects with Southbridge Street; thence to and
by the centre of Southbridge Street to the main
track of the Boston and Albany Railroad; thence
by the main track of the Boston and Albany Railroad to the main track of the Norwich and Worcester Railroad near the Junction Depot; thence by
the main track of the Norwich and Worcester Railroad to the boundary line between Worcester and
Auburn; thence by the boundary line between Worcester and Auburn to the boundary line between
Worcester and Leicester; thence by the boundary
line between Worcester and Leicester to the centre
of Leicester Street; thence to and by the centre of
Leicester Street to Main Street; thence to and by
the centre of Main Street to the point of beginning,
and contains 1396 voters.

Boundary of
Ward Six.

WARD NO. SEVEN.

Beginning at the centre of Main Street at a point Boundary of Ward Seven. opposite the centre of Chatham Street; thence to and by the centre of Main Street to Leicester Street; thence to and by the centre of Leicester Street to the boundary line between Worcester and Leicester; thence by the boundary line between Worcester and Leicester to Fowler Street; thence easterly in a direct line to a point where Chandler Street intersects with June Street; thence to and by the centre of Chandler Street to a point opposite the centre of Newbury Street; thence to and by the centre of Newbury Street to a point opposite the centre of Chatham Street; thence to and by the centre of Chatham Street to Main Street; thence in a direct line to the point of beginning, and contains 1346 voters.

WARD NO. EIGHT.

Beginning at the centre of Main Street at a point Boundary of Ward Eight. opposite the centre of Chatham Street; thence to and by the centre of Chatham Street to Newbury Street; thence to and by the centre of Newbury Street to Chandler Street; thence to and by the centre of Chandler Street to a point opposite the centre of June Street; thence westerly in a direct line to Fowler Street at its junction with the boundary line between Worcester and Leicester; thence by the boundary line between Worcester and Leicester to the northwest corner of the City; thence by the boundary line between Worcester and Paxton and Worcester and Holden to its junction with Cataract Street; thence in a direct line to a point on the east side of Agricultural Street at the southwest corner of the grounds of the Agricultural Society; thence in a direct line to William Street; thence to and by the centre of William Street to Chestnut Street; thence to and by the centre of Chestnut Street to Walnut Street; thence to and by the centre of Walnut Street to Main Street; thence to and by the centre of Main Street to the point of beginning, and contains 1353 voters.

Repeal. SECT. 2. All ordinances or parts of ordinances inconsistent herewith, are hereby repealed.

When to take effect. SECT. 3. This ordinance shall take effect on and after the first day of December, A. D. one thousand eight hundred and seventy-five.

PASSED Nov. 16, 1875.

ORDER.

_____

Resolved, That the legal centre of the city shall be the point formed by the intersection of the south line of Front street and the east line of Main street; and that all circles, of whatever radius, used for denoting distance from the central portion of the city shall have a common centre at said point.

And it is further ordered, That all orders which in any way refer to a mile circle of any other radius used for denoting distance as above described, shall be so amended that the circle intended shall be, in each case, a circle of the given radius having the said point for a centre.

ADOPTED MAY 20, 1872.

STATUTES ADOPTED.

The following Statutes were adopted in the Ordinances passed April 16, 1867.

Relating to the election of city officers, General Statutes, c. 19, sections 6 to 10, inclusive.

Relating to the holding of other offices by the Mayor and Aldermen, General Statutes, c. 19, section 12.

Relating to laying out and grading sidewalks, General Statutes, c. 45, sections 7 and 8.

Relating to shade trees, General Statutes c. 46, section 9.

Relating to sewers and drains, General Statutes c. 48, sections 3 to 6, inclusive. Section 3 was repealed by St. 1869, c. 111. (See St. 1878, c. 184, 232. St. 1879, c. 85.)

Relating to weighing hay and other articles, General Statutes c. 49, sections 72 to 75, inclusive.

Relating to nuisances, General Statutes c. 87, sections 1 to 5, inclusive.

Relating to steam engines, furnaces and boilers, General Statutes c. 88, sections 33 to 40, inclusive.

Relating to stationary engines, St. of 1862, c. 74.

Relating to the sealing of weights and measures, St. 1863, c. 179. See St. 1876, c. 123. St. 1877, c. 151.

Since then the following Statutes have been adopted:

Relating to the fire department. St. 1868, c. 195; accepted Sept. 28, 1868.

Relating to sidewalks. St. 1869, c. 390; accepted Sept. 20, 1869.

An act for the prevention of fires. St. 1872, c. 243; accepted Nov. 8, 1880.

An act to establish a board of health. St. 1877, c. 133; accepted by the inhabitants, Nov. 6, 1877.

Relating to inspectors of elections. St. 1877, c. 209; accepted Oct. 15, 1877.

Relating to the inspection of buildings. St. 1878, c. 47; accepted Nov. 22, 1880.

Relating to the apportionment of sewer and sidewalk assessments. St. 1878, c. 249; accepted Nov. 8. 1880.

CITY COUNCIL,

FROM

1848 TO 1880.

1848.

Mayor.

LEVI LINCOLN.

Aldermen.

Ward 1. PARLEY GODDARD,
2. BENJAMIN F. THOMAS,
3. JOHN W. LINCOLN,
4. JAMES S. WOODWORTH,
5. WILLIAM B. FOX,
6. JAMES ESTABROOK,
7. ISAAC DAVIS,
8. STEPHEN SALISBURY

City Clerk.

CHARLES A. HAMILTON.

Common Council.

Ward 1. FREEMAN UPHAM,
JOHN SUTTON,
SAMUEL B. SCOTT.

2. HORACE CHENERY,
EDWARD LAMB,
CALVIN BRIGHAM.

3. BENJAMIN F. HEYWOOD,
CHARLES BOWEN,
JOHN GATES.

4. ALVIN ALLEN.
DARIUS RICE,
STEPHEN BARTLETT.

5. ISAAC GODDARD,
JOSIAH G. PERRY,
BENJAMIN F. STOWELL.

6. EDWIN DRAPER,
ADOLPHUS MORSE,
NATHANIEL BROOKS.

7. ALEXANDER H. BULLOCK,
ALBERT CURTIS,
DANIEL GODDARD.

8. WILLIAM T. MERRIFIELD,
CALVIN FOSTER,
THOS. CHAMBERLAIN, *Pres't.*

WILLIAM A. SMITH, *Clerk.*

1849.

Mayor.

HENRY CHAPIN.

Aldermen.

Ward 1. WILLIAM A. WHEELER,
2. WARREN LAZELL,
3. WILLIAM A. DRAPER,
4. CHARLES G. PRENTICE,
5. AUSTIN G. FITCH,
6. CHARLES WHITE,
7. PETER C. BACON,
8. BENJAMIN FLAGG.

City Clerk.

CHARLES A. HAMILTON.

Common Council.

Ward 1. FREEMAN UPHAM,
LUTHER WHITE,
NATHAN MUZZY.

2. JOHN H. BROOKS,
THOMAS H. RICE,
CHARLES WASHBURN.

3. WILLIAM DICKINSON,
L. W. STURTEVANT,
DANIEL HARRINGTON.

4. ALVIN ALLEN,
DARIUS RICE,
JOSEPH PRATT.

5. BENJAMIN GODDARD, 2D,
ISAAC GODDARD,
DAVID WOODWARD.

6. ADOLPHUS MORSE,
EDWIN DRAPER,
JOHN F. GLEASON.

7. ALEXANDER DEWITT,
ERASTUS TUCKER,
JAMES M. FITCH.

8. ALBERT TOLMAN,
WILLIAM G. MOORE,
JONAS M. MILES, *Pres't.*

WILLIAM A. SMITH, *Clerk.*

1850.

Mayor.
HENRY CHAPIN.

Aldermen.
Ward 1. GEORGE W. RUSSELL,
2. WARREN LAZELL,
3. WILLIAM DICKINSON,
4. JOSEPH PRATT,
5. DAVID WOODWARD,
6. CHARLES WHITE,
7. ANTHONY CHASE,
8. JONAS M. MILES.

City Clerk.
CHARLES A. HAMILTON.

Common Council.
Ward 1. NATHAN MUZZY,
JOSEPH LEWIS,
FREEMAN UPHAM.*

2. CHARLES WASHBURN, *Pres't.*
LEE SPRAGUE,
JOHN H. BROOKS.

3. DANIEL HARRINGTON,
L. W. STURTEVANT,†
HENRY PRENTICE.

4. CALVIN NEWTON,
JOHN P. SOUTHGATE,
CALVIN L. PROUTY.

5. HENRY J. HOWLAND,
WILLIAM H. HARRIS,
DANIEL S. BURGESS.

6. ADOLPHUS MORSE,
JOHN F. GLEASON,
JOSEPH D. BRIGHAM.

7. ERASTUS TUCKER,
BENJAMIN GODDARD, 3D,
ALBERT BROWN.

8. ALBERT TOLMAN,
HENRY H. CHAMBERLAIN,
WILLIAM WORKMAN.‡

WILLIAM A. SMITH, *Clerk.*

* Declined, G. W. Wilder elected.
† Declined, Franklin Hall elected.
‡ Declined, Thomas Drew elected.

1851.

Mayor.
PETER C. BACON.

Aldermen.
Ward 1. GEORGE W. RUSSELL,
2. ICHABOD WASHBURN,
3. DANIEL HARRINGTON,
4. JOSEPH PRATT,
5. DAVID WOODWARD,
6. ADOLPHUS MORSE,*
7. JOHN M. EARLE,
8. JONAS M. MILES.

City Clerk.
CHARLES A. HAMILTON.

Common Council.
Ward 1. NATHAN MUZZY,
JOSEPH LEWIS,
ALEXANDER THAYER.

2. CHARLES WASHBURN, *Pres't.*
LEE SPRAGUE,
BENJAMIN B. OTIS.

3. ADAM DAWSON,
WILLIAM B. MAXWELL,
GILL VALENTINE.

4. CALVIN NEWTON,
JOHN P. SOUTHGATE,
JOHN F. BURBANK.

5. DANIEL S. BURGESS,
HENRY S. WASHBURN,
BRIGHAM GOSS.

6. JOHN F. GLEASON,
JOSEPH D. BRIGHAM,
PEREGRINE B. GILBERT.

7. ERASTUS TUCKER,
NATHAN AINSWORTH,
SAMUEL H. COLTON.

8. ALBERT TOLMAN,
HENRY H. CHAMBERLAIN,
JONAS HARTSHORN.

WILLIAM A. SMITH, *Clerk.*

* Resigned, Charles White elected.

1852.

Mayor.
PETER C. BACON.

Aldermen.
Ward 1. FREEMAN UPHAM,
   2. EDWARD LAMB.
   3. HENRY PRENTICE,
   4. CALVIN NEWTON,
   5. DAVID WOODWARD,
   6. JOHN F. GLEASON,
   7. ISAAC DAVIS,
   8. WM. DICKINSON.*

City Clerk.
CHARLES A. HAMILTON.

Common Council.
Ward 1. ALEXANDER THAYER,
    HENRY EARLE,
    SAMUEL A. PORTER.

   2. GEORGE W. RUGG,
    JOHN B. PRATT,
    CHARLES DAVIS.†

   3. GILL VALENTINE,
    CHARLES BOWEN,
    GERRY VALENTINE.

   4. JOHN F. BURBANK, *Pres't.*
    SAMUEL D. HARDING,
    MOSES SPOONER.

   5. DAVID D. STOWELL,
    HENRY MURRAY,
    BRIGHAM GOSS. ‡

   6. JAMES H. WALL,
    MARSHALL S. BALLORD,
    LEVI BARKER.

   7. TIMOTHY S. STONE,
    SAMUEL H. COLTON,
    DAVID W. COOKE.

   8. WILLIAM M. BICKFORD,
    ROSWELL P. ANGIER,
    JOSEPH WALKER, JR.
    WARREN ADAMS, *Clerk.*

* Resigned.
† Declined, Benj. Walker elected.
‡ Declined, Daniel S. Burgess elected.

1853.

Mayor.
JOHN S. C. KNOWLTON.

Aldermen.
Ward 1. WILLIAM A. WILLIAMS,
   2. EDWARD EARLE,
   3. GILL VALENTINE,
   4. SAMUEL D. HARDING,
   5. PHINEHAS CRANDALL,
   6. MOSES D. PHILLIPS,
   7. CHARLES WHITE,
   8. BENJAMIN FLAGG.

City Clerk.
CHARLES A. HAMILTON.

Common Council.
Ward 1. HENRY EARLE,
    R. O. FORBUSH,
    SAMUEL A. PORTER.

   2. CHARLES WASHBURN,
    GEORGE W. RUGG,*
    TIMOTHY BANCROFT.

   3. WM. N. GREEN, *Pres't.*
    GERRY VALENTINE,
    SAMUEL T. FIELD.

   4. JAMES S. WOODWORTH,
    LOISON D. TOWNE,
    PLINY HOLBROOK.

   5. EZRA P. CLARK,
    GARDNER MCFARLAND,
    HENRY MURRAY.

   6. MARSHAL S. BALLORD,
    JAMES H. WALL,
    LEVI BARKER.

   7. SAMUEL B. DENNIS,
    JOHN A. HUNT.
    SAMUEL H. COLTON.

   8. JOSEPH WALKER, JR.
    WM. M. BICKFORD,
    ROSWELL P. ANGIER.
    LEWIS A. MAYNARD, *Clerk.*

* Declined, Calvin Knowlton elected.

1854.

Mayor.

JOHN S. C. KNOWLTON.

Aldermen.

Ward 1. WILLIAM A. WILLIAMS.
    2. CHARLES WASHBURN,
    3. HARTLEY WILLIAMS,
    4. SAMUEL D. HARDING,
    5. MOSES D. PHILLIPS,
    6. JAMES H. WALL,
    7. ELI THAYER,
    8. BENJAMIN WALKER.

City Clerk.

CHARLES A. HAMILTON.

Common Council.

Ward 1. SAMUEL A. PORTER,
    GERRY VALENTINE,
    FRANCIS HOVEY.

    2. ICHABOD WASHBURN,
    THOMAS H. RICE,
    EDWARD LAMB.

    3. HENRY TOLMAN,
    LYSANDER CHANDLER,
    HENRY PRENTICE.*

    4. JAMES S. WOODWORTH,
    LOISON D. TOWNE,
    PHILIP LOTHROP.

    5. WILLARD BROWN,
    FRANCIS STRONG,
    WILLIAM S. LINCOLN.

    6. JOSIAH W. ALLEN,
    JAS. ESTABROOK, *Pres't.*
    JOSEPH H. WALKER.

    7. CALVIN FOSTER,
    JONAS HARTSHORN,
    ELIJAH B. STODDARD.

    8. JOSEPH WALKER, JR.
    GEORGE HOBBS,
    HENRY GOULDING.

WILLIAM A. SMITH, *Clerk.*

1855.

Mayor.

GEO. W. RICHARDSON.

Aldermen.

Ward 1. HENRY EARL,
    2. SAMUEL DAVIS,
    3. WILLIAM T. MERRIFIELD,
    4. JOHN P. SOUTHGATE,
    5. WILLIAM H. HARRIS,
    6. JAMES H. WALL,
    7. ALVIN WAITE,
    8. HENRY GOULDING.

City Clerk.

CHARLES A. HAMILTON.*

Common Council.

Ward 1. JOHN GATES,
    ALEXANDER THAYER,
    ALEXANDER PUTNAM.

    2. SAMUEL A. KNOX,
    HORACE CHENERY,
    OZIAS HUDSON.†

    3. REUBEN RANDALL,
    LEONARD POOLE,
    HENRY TOLMAN.

    4. FRANCIS HARRINGTON,
    LEWIS STURTEVANT,
    NATHAN WASHBURN.

    5. FRANCIS STRONG,
    GEORGE E. WYMAN,
    EDWARD S. STEBBINS.

    6. LORIN WETHERELL,
    JOHN B. DEXTER,
    THOMAS PIERCE.

    7. GEORGE M. RICE, *Pres't.*
    HENRY GRIFFIN,
    THOMAS EARLE.

    8. JOSEPH D. DANIELS,
    PARLEY HAMMOND,
    JOSEPH P. CHENEY.

WILLIAM A. SMITH, *Clerk.*

---

* Declined, Reuben Randall elected.

* Resigned, Samuel Smith elected.

1856.

Mayor.
ISAAC DAVIS.

Aldermen.
Ward 1. BENJ. F. HEYWOOD,
  2. JOSEPH P. HALE,*
  3. HENRY PRENTICE,
  4. JAMES S. WOODWORTH,
  5. SAMUEL V. STONE,
  6. CALVIN WILLARD,†
  7. CALVIN FOSTER,
  8. WILLIAM S. LINCOLN.

City Clerk.
SAMUEL SMITH.

Common Council.
Ward 1. DAVID HITCHCOCK,‡
    AUSTIN FLINT,
    GEORGE H. TUFTS.

  2. RANSOM M. GOULD,
    GEORGE SPAULDING,
    ORAN A. KELLEY.

  3. JASON TEMPLE,
    HENRY D. STONE,
    CHARLES BOWEN.

  4. SAMUEL D. HARDING,
    CHARLES B. PRATT,
    MOSES TAFT.

  5. JOHN S. GUSTIN,
    LEVI BARKER,
    GEORGE H. WARD.

  6. DANA H. FITCH,
    LORIN WETHERELL,
    THOMAS PIERCE.

  7. GEORGE M. RICE, *Pres't,*
    ALBERT P. WARE,
    JOHN C. JAQUES.

  8. WILLIAM DICKINSON,
    CHARLES W. FREELAND,
    JOSEPH P. CHENEY.

  • WILLIAM A. SMITH, *Clerk.*

* Resigned, Edward Lamb elected.
† Declined, James H. Wall elected.
‡ Resigned, Henry Earl elected.

1857.

Mayor.
GEO. W. RICHARDSON.

Aldermen.
Ward 1. HENRY EARL,
  2. WILLIAM A. WHEELER,
  3. HENRY PRENTICE,
  4. JOHN P. SOUTHGATE,
  5. FRANCIS STRONG,
  6. ALBERT CURTIS,
  7. CHARLES WHITE,
  8. HENRY GOULDING.

City Clerk.
SAMUEL SMITH.

Common Council.
Ward 1. AUSTIN FLINT,
    HENRY P. NICHOLS,
    CHARLES H. BALLARD.

  2. ORAN A. KELLEY,
    RANSOM M. GOULD,*
    DANIEL TAINTER.

  3. JASON TEMPLE,
    HENRY D. STONE,
    CALVIN E. PRATT.

  4. CHARLES B. PRATT,
    RUFUS O. WILLIAMS,
    ELISHA F. WITT.

  5. JOHN S. GUSTIN,
    PATRICK O'KEEFE,
    SAMUEL V. STONE.

  6. EDWIN DRAPER,
    SYLVANUS PRATT,
    JOEL DAVIS.

  7. GEORGE M. RICE, *Pres't,*
    AURY G. COES,
    HORATIO N. TOWER.

  8. WILLIAM M. BICKFORD,
    JOSHUA M. C. ARMSBY,
    SAMUEL H. LEONARD.

  WILLIAM A. SMITH, *Clerk.*

* Resigned, vacancy not filled.

1858.

Mayor.
ISAAC DAVIS.

Aldermen.
Ward 1. BENJAMIN F. HEYWOOD,
2. DRAPER RUGGLES,
3. HENRY PRENTICE,*
4. PLINY HOLBROOK,
5. WILLIAM B. FOX, JR.,
6. THOMAS PIERCE,
7. D. WALDO LINCOLN,
8. DAVID S. MESSINGER.

City Clerk.
SAMUEL SMITH.

Common Council.
Ward 1. CHARLES H. BALLARD,
T. W. HAMMOND,†
F. C. BIGELOW.‡

2. JOSHUA M. C. ARMSBY,
MOORE M. CHAFFIN,
LUCIUS W. POND.

3. SAMUEL C. RICHARDS,
JOHN S. GUSTIN,
LYMAN BROWN.

4. ELISHA F. WITT,
SAMUEL HATHAWAY,
ALVIN ALLEN.

5. LEVI BARKER,
GEORGE H. WARD,
SAMUEL V. STONE.

6. JAMES H. WALL,
JOSEPH BOYDEN,
GEORGE S. BARTON.

7. ELIJAH B. STODDARD, *Pres't.*
AURY G. COES,
EDWIN MORSE.

8. HENRY C. RICE,
JOSEPH D. DANIELS.
MARTIN LATHE.

WILLIAM A. SMITH, *Clerk.*

1859.

Mayor.
ALEXANDER H. BULLOCK.

Aldermen.
Ward 1. ALEXANDER THAYER,
2. JOSHUA M. C. ARMSBY,
3. JONAS BARTLETT,
4. PLINY HOLBROOK,
5. ISAAC GODDARD,
6. LORIN COES,
7. D. WALDO LINCOLN.
8. DAVID S. MESSINGER.

City Clerk.
SAMUEL SMITH.

Common Council.
Ward 1. TIMOTHY W. HAMMOND,
HENRY P. NICHOLS,
RANSOM M. GOULD.

2. LUCIUS W. POND,
A. B. R. SPRAGUE,
JOHN BARNARD.

3. LYMAN BROWN,
JAMES E. ESTABROOK,
WALTER HENRY.

4. CHARLES B. PRATT,
WILLIAM ADAMS,
APPLETON DADMUN.

5. JOHN SIMMONS,
HENRY MURRAY,
SAMUEL V. STONE.

6. EDWIN DRAPER,
GEORGE S. BARTON,
DANA H. FITCH.

7. EDWIN MORSE,
AURY G. COES,
SAMUEL R. HEYWOOD.

8. JOHN W. WETHERELL, *Pres't.*
GEO. A. CHAMBERLIN,
WILLIAM GREENLEAF.

WILLIAM A. SMITH, *Clerk.*

* Resigned, Jonas Bartlett elected.
† Resigned, Ransom M. Gould elected.
‡ Resigned, Pardon W. Aldrich elected.

1860.

Mayor.

WILLIAM W. RICE.

Aldermen.

Ward 1. ALEXANDER THAYER,
  2. ALBERT TOLMAN,
  3. ASA L. BURBANK,
  4. FRANCIS HARRINGTON,
  5. ISAAC GODDARD,
  6. EDWIN DRAPER,
  7. SAMUEL R. HEYWOOD,
  8. DAVID S. MESSINGER.

City Clerk.

SAMUEL SMITH.

Common Council.

Ward 1. HENRY B. HAKES,
   GERRY VALENTINE,
   SAMUEL E. STAPLES.

  2. GEORGE R. PECKHAM,
   A. B. R. SPRAGUE,
   EDWIN A. MUZZY.

  3. JAMES E. ESTABROOK,
   LYMAN BROWN,
   DENNIS G. TEMPLE. -

  4. MOSES TAFT,
   CHARLES B. PRATT,
   CHARLES S. CHILDS.

  5. SIMEON CLAPP,
   CHARLES F. WASHBURN,
   GEORGE CROMPTON. .

  6. DANA H. FITCH,
   HENRY GODDARD,
   JOHN W. JORDAN.

  7. JOSEPH H. WALKER, *Pres't.*
   AARON G. WALKER,
   AURY G. COES.

  8. RICHARD BALL,
   ELBRIDGE BOYDEN,
   EPHRAIM F. CHAMBERLAIN.

WILLIAM A. SMITH, *Clerk.*

1861.

Mayor.

ISAAC DAVIS.

Aldermen.

Ward 1. MERRICK BEMIS,
  2. HARRISON BLISS,
  3. LEONARD W. STURTEVANT.
  4. CHARLES B. PRATT,
  5. ISAAC GODDARD,
  6. STEPHEN TAFT,
  7. SAMUEL R. HEYWOOD,
  8. GEORGE HOBBS.

City Clerk.

SAMUEL SMITH.

Common Council.

Ward 1. ALEX. Y. THOMPSON,
   J. WALDO DENNY,
   JOSIAH H. CLARK.

  2. WALTER BIGELOW,
   SILAS J. BRIMHALL,
   THEOD. M. WOODWARD.

  3. JAMES E. ESTABROOK, *Pres't.*
   WALTER HENRY. .
   FRANCIS B. NORTON.

  4. APPLETON DADMUN,
   FRANK H. KELLEY,
   MICHAEL S. McCONVILLE.

  5. GEORGE CROMPTON,
   JAMES MELANEFY,
   RICHARD BARKER.

  6. JOSIAH W. ALLEN,
   LORIN WETHERELL,
   FREDERICK W. TOWNSEND.

  7. AARON G. WALKER,
   JAMES F. ESTEY,
   HENRY C. RICE.

  8. FRANCIS H. DEWEY,
   RICHARD BALL,
   SAMUEL A. PORTER.

JOHN A. DANA, *Clerk.*

1862.

Mayor.

P. EMORY ALDRICH.

Aldermen.

Ward 1. MERRICK BEMIS,
2. LUCIUS W. POND,
3. ADAM HARRINGTON,
4. SAMUEL D. HARDING,
5. FRANCIS STRONG,
6. CHARLES B. PRATT,
7. GEORGE CHANDLER,
8. BENJAMIN WALKER.

City Clerk.

SAMUEL SMITH.

Common Council.

Ward 1. ALEXANDER Y. THOMPSON,
LEONARD R. HUDSON,
CHARLES WHITTEMORE.

2. PHILIP L. MOEN, *Pres't*,
PHINEHAS BALL,
SILAS J. BRIMHALL.

3. FRED. B. NORTON,
LYMAN BROWN,
WALTER HENRY.

4. APPLETON DADMUN,
FRANK H. KELLEY,
SAMUEL R. LELAND.

5. EDWIN C. CLEVELAND,
HUGH DOHERTY,
RICHARD BARKER.

6. HENRY GODDARD,
JOHN W. JORDAN,
JOHN R. GREENE.

7. JULIUS E. TUCKER,
JONATHAN F. ESTEY,
GEORGE S. BARTON.

8. CALEB B. METCALF,
ADDISON PALMER,
AUGUSTUS N. CURRIER.
JOHN A. DANA, *Clerk.*

1863.

Mayor.

D. WALDO LINCOLN.

Aldermen.

Ward 1. MERRICK BEMIS,*
2. HARRISON BLISS,
3. LEONARD W. STURTEVANT,
4. FRANK H. KELLEY,
5. GEORGE CROMPTON,
6. CHARLES B. PRATT,†
7. ELIJAH B. STODDARD,
8. GEORGE HOBBS.

City Clerk.

SAMUEL SMITH.

Common Council.

Ward 1. A. McFARLAND DAVIS,
GEORGE A. GATES,
GEORGE F. RICE.

2. PHILIP L. MOEN, *Pres't*,
PHINEHAS BALL,‡
GEORGE R. PECKHAM.

3. S. P. TWISS,§
J. BROWN ALDEN,
JAMES RADIGAN.

4. SAMUEL R. LELAND,
DANIEL H. O'NEIL,
GEORGE H. CLARK.

5. RICHARD BARKER,
HUGH DOHERTY,
DWIGHT NEWBURY.

6. JOHN R. GREENE,
WILLIAM H. JACOBS,
CHARLES WOOD.

7. GEORGE S. BARTON,
JULIUS E. TUCKER,
RUSSELL R. SHEPARD.

8. RICHARD BALL,
DEXTER RICE,
WILLIAM WORKMAN.
JOHN A. DANA, *Clerk.*

* Resigned, Chas. A. Wheeler elected.
† Resigned, Stephen Taft elected.
‡ Resigned.
§ Resigned, Rolla N. Start elected.

1864.

Mayor.

D. WALDO LINCOLN.

Aldermen.

Ward 1. CHARLES A. WHEELER,
2. HARRISON BLISS,
3. CALVIN DYER,
4. FRANK H. KELLEY,
5. GEORGE CROMPTON,
6. STEPHEN TAFT,
7. ELIJAH B. STODDARD,
8. GEORGE HOBBS.

City Clerk.

SAMUEL SMITH.

Common Council.

Ward 1. GEORGE F. RICE,
APPLETON DADMUN,
CHARLES WHITTEMORE.

2. PHILIP L. MOEN,
GEORGE G. BURBANK,
GEORGE R. PECKHAM.

3. ROLLA N. START,
LYMAN BROWN,
PATRICK NUGENT.

4. MOSES TAFT,
GEORGE H. CLARK,
PATRICK BURKE.

5. ELISHA A. HARKNESS,
PRENTICE A. THOMPSON,
BERNARD CARROLL.

6. JOHN R. GREENE,
WILLIAM H. JACOBS,
CHARLES WOOD.

7. JULIUS E. TUCKER,
GEORGE S. BARTON,
RUSSELL R. SHEPARD.

8. RICHARD BALL, *Pres't,*
JOSEPH D. DANIELS,
DEXTER RICE.

JOHN A. DANA, *Clerk.*

1865.

Mayor.

PHINEHAS BALL.

Aldermen.

Ward 1. HENRY B. HAKES,
2. WALTER BIGELOW,
3. CALVIN DYER,
4. GEORGE W. RUGG,
5. E. C. CLEVELAND,
6. HENRY GODDARD,
7. EDWIN MORSE,
8. HARRISON BLISS.

City Clerk.

SAMUEL SMITH.

Common Council.

Ward 1. DEWITT FISHER,
EDWARD L. DAVIS,
LEONARD R. HUDSON.

2. GEORGE R. PECKHAM,
LUTHER ROSS,
LUTHER PHILLIPS.

3. FRANKLIN B. NORTON,
PATRICK NUGENT,
LYMAN BROWN.

4. OSGOOD BRADLEY, JR.,
ANDREW ATHY,
WILLIAM B. MCIVER.

5. E. A. HARKNESS,
JOHN L. MURPHY,
SALISBURY HYDE.

6. JONATHAN C. FRENCH,
GEORGE T. MURDOCK,
GEORGE S. HOPPIN.

7. JULIUS E. TUCKER,
WILLIAM E. STARR, *Pres't,*
SAMUEL WINSLOW.

8. GEORGE W. RUSSELL,
ELBRIDGE BOYDEN,
D. A. HAWKINS, JR.

JOHN A. DANA, *Clerk.*

1866.

Mayor.

JAMES B. BLAKE.

Aldermen.

Ward 1. JEROME MARBLE,
2. OLIVER K. EARLE,
3. HENRY B. HAKES,
4. H. HAMLIN HOUGHTON,
5. GEORGE A. BROWN,
6. JONATHAN C. FRENCH,
7. AURY G. COES,
8. FRANCIS H. DEWEY.

City Clerk.

SAMUEL SMITH.

Common Council.

Ward 1. STEPHEN SALISBURY, JR.,
DANIEL A. HAWKINS,
AUSTIN L. ROGERS.

2. GEORGE W. PAUL,
HENRY C. WILSON,
LUTHER ROSS.

3. EDWARD L. DAVIS,
WALTER HENRY,
SAMUEL E. HILDRETH.

4. OSGOOD BRADLEY, JR.,
JAMES MCFARLAND,
JOHN L. MURPHY.

5. SALISBURY HYDE,
EVERETT W. FRENCH,
ALBERT A. GORDON.

6. GEORGE S. HOPPIN,
DANA H. FITCH,
H. S. WHITTEMORE.

7. JOHN S. BALDWIN,
AARON G. WALKER,
EDWIN T. MARBLE.

8. WM. E. STARR, *Pres't.*
SAMUEL WINSLOW,
ADDISON PALMER.

HENRY L. SHUMWAY, *Clerk.*

1867.

Mayor.

JAMES B. BLAKE.

Aldermen.

Ward 1. EDWARD KENDALL.
2. OLIVER K. EARLE,
3. SAMUEL E. HILDRETH,
4. H. HAMLIN HOUGHTON,
5. SIMEON CLAPP,*
6. DANA H. FITCH,
7. JOHN D. LOVELL,
8. GEORGE S. BARTON.

City Clerk.

SAMUEL SMITH.

Common Council.

Ward 1. STEPHEN SALISBURY, JR.,
DANIEL A. HAWKINS,
AUSTIN L. ROGERS.

2. GEORGE W. PAUL,
HENRY C. WILSON,
LUTHER ROSS.

3. WALTER HENRY.
LEONARD R. HUDSON,
LYMAN BROWN.

4. PATRICK O'KEEFE,
GEORGE H. CLARK,
VERNON A. LADD.

5. DEXTER H. PERRY,
JOSIAH W. ALLEN,
DAVID M. WOODWARD.

6. JOHN DEAN,
HENRY S. WHITTEMORE,
JOHN L. WATERS.

7. EDWIN T. MARBLE,
JOHN S. BALDWIN,
J. ORLANDO BEMIS.

8. HENRY A. MARSH.
RANSOM M. GOULD,
EDWARD L. DAVIS, *Pres't.*

HENRY L. SHUMWAY, *Clerk.*

* Died May 31, 1867.

24

1868.

Mayor.

JAMES B. BLAKE.

Aldermen.

Ward 1. EDWARD KENDALL,
    2. ALBERT TOLMAN,
    3. SAMUEL E. HILDRETH,
    4. H. HAMLIN HOUGHTON,
    5. EDWIN C. CLEVELAND,
    6. HENRY GODDARD,
    7. JOHN D. LOVELL,
    8. GEORGE S. BARTON.

City Clerk.

SAMUEL SMITH.

Common Council.

Ward 1. STEPHEN SALISBURY, JR., *Pres't.*
      TIMOTHY W. HAMMOND,
      NATHANIEL PAINE.

    2. GEORGE W. PAUL,
      HENRY C. WILSON,
      LUTHER ROSS.

    3. WALTER HENRY,
      LEONARD R. HUDSON,
      GEORGE F. HEWETT.

    4. PATRICK O'KEEFE,
      GEORGE H. CLARK,
      VERNON A. LADD.

    5. DEXTER H. PERRY,
      A. B. COUCH,
      DAVID M. WOODWARD.

    6. JOHN DEAN,
      HENRY S. WHITTEMORE,
      JOHN L. WATERS,

    7. EDWIN T. MARBLE,
      JOHN S. BALDWIN,
      OBADIAH B. HADWEN.

    8. HENRY A. MARSH,
      RANSOM M. GOULD,
      GERRY HUTCHINSON.

HENRY L. SHUMWAY, *Clerk.*

1869.

Mayor.

JAMES B. BLAKE.

Aldermen.

Ward 1. EDWARD KENDALL,
    2. ALBERT TOLMAN,
    3. THOMAS HARRINGTON,
    4. H. HAMLIN HOUGHTON,
    5. EDWIN C. CLEVELAND,
    6. HENRY GODDARD,
    7. EDWIN T. MARBLE,
    8. GEORGE S. BARTON.

City Clerk.

SAMUEL SMITH.

Common Council.

Ward 1. JOSEPH CHASE,
      TIMOTHY W. HAMMOND,
      NATHANIEL PAINE.

    2. GEORGE W. PAUL,
      R. E. BLAKE,
      LUTHER ROSS.

    3. R. H. CHAMBERLAIN,
      LEONARD R. HUDSON,
      GEORGE F. HEWETT.

    4. ANDREW ATHY,
      MICHAEL O'DRISCOLL,
      VERNON A. LADD.

    5. SAMUEL V. STONE, *Pres't,*
      A. B. COUCH,
      DAVID M. WOODWARD.

    6. SAMUEL HOUGHTON,
      CHARLES G. REED,
      JOHN L. WATERS.

    7. JOSEPH B. KNOX,
      JOHN S. BALDWIN,
      OBADIAH B. HADWEN.

    8. ADDISON PALMER,
      SUMNER PRATT,
      GERRY HUTCHINSON.

HENRY L. SHUMWAY, *Clerk.*

1870.

Mayor.

JAMES B. BLAKE.*

Aldermen.

Ward 1. EDWARD KENDALL,
2. LEWIS BARNARD,
3. THOMAS HARRINGTON,
4. FRANK H. KELLEY,
5. EDWIN C. CLEVELAND,
6. JOHN W. JORDAN,
7. EDWIN T. MARBLE,
8. GEORGE S. BARTON.

City Clerk.

SAMUEL SMITH.

Common Council.

Ward 1. JOSEPH CHASE,
TIMOTHY W. HAMMOND,
DANIEL W. KNOWLTON.

2. WM. ALLEN,
R. E. BLAKE,
LUTHER ROSS.

3. R. H. CHAMBERLAIN,
WALTER HENRY,
GEORGE F. HEWETT.

4. ANDREW ATHY,
MICHAEL O'DRISCOLL,
A. H. WARD.

5. O. L. HATCH,
CHAS. W. PARKER,
CALEB COLVIN.

6. SAMUEL HOUGHTON,
CHARLES G. REED, *Pres't.*
L. HENRY WELLS.

7. JOSEPH B. KNOX,
EDWIN AMES,
SAMUEL BROWN.

8. ADDISON PALMER,
SUMNER PRATT,
GERRY HUTCHINSON.

HENRY L. SHUMWAY, *Clerk.*

* Re-elected Dec. 12, 1870. Died Dec. 18, 1870. Henry Chapin elected by the City Council, Mayor "*ad interim*," Dec. 19, 1870.

1871.

Mayor.

EDWARD EARLE.†

Aldermen.

Ward 1. AUGUSTUS B. R. SPRAGUE.
2. LEWIS BARNARD,
3. GILBERT J. RUGG,
4. FRANK H. KELLEY,
5. HORACE WYMAN,
6. JOHN W. JORDAN,
7. EDWIN T. MARBLE,
8. GEORGE S. BARTON.

City Clerk.

SAMUEL SMITH.

Common Council.

Ward 1. JOSEPH CHASE,
SIMON E. COMBS,
DAN'L W. KNOWLTON.

2. WM. ALLEN,
AARON G. WALKER,
LUTHER ROSS.

3. WALTER HENRY,
GEORGE F. HEWETT,
CHARLES W. WENTWORTH.

4. ANDREW ATHY,
CHARLES S. CHILDS,
MICHAEL O'DRISCOLL.

5. O. L. HATCH,
CHAS. W. PARKER,
MORRIS MELAVEN.

6. JOSEPH H. WALKER,
CHARLES G. REED, *Pres't.*
L. HENRY WELLS.

7. CALVIN L. HARTSHORN,
EDWIN AMES,
SAMUEL BROWN.

8. E. H. TOWNE,
SUMNER PRATT,
GERRY HUTCHINSON.

HENRY L. SHUMWAY, *Clerk.*

† Elected Jan. 30, 1871, to fill vacancy.

1872.

Mayor.

GEORGE F. VERRY.

Aldermen.

Ward 1. Emory Banister,
    2. Joseph Burrough,
    3. Gilbert J. Rugg,
    4. Samuel D. Harding,
    5. Horace Wyman,
    6. Henry H. Chamberlin,
    7. Edwin T. Marble,
    8. George R. Spurr.

City Clerk.

Samuel Smith.

Common Council.

Ward 1. Joseph Chase.
    Edward R. Fiske,
    John W. Howe.

    2. Wm. Allen,
    Parritt Blaisdell,
    Luther Ross.

    3. Samuel McFadden,
    George F. Hewett,
    Chas. W. Wentworth.

    4. Andrew Athy,
    Patrick D. Conlin,
    Charles S. Childs.

    5. John J. O'Gorman,
    John Cove,
    Morris Melaven.

    6. Joseph H. Walker,
    Charles G. Reed, *Pres't.*
    Dorrance S. Goddard.

    7. Calvin L. Hartshorn,
    Edwin Ames,
    Amariah B. Lovell.

    8. E. H. Towne,
    Sumner Pratt,
    Charles G. Parker.

    Henry L. Shumway, *Clerk.*

1873.

Mayor.

CLARK JILLSON

Aldermen.

Ward 1. George S. Hoppin,
    2. Joseph Burrough,
    3. William H. Jourdan,
    4. Samuel D. Harding,
    5. Ransom C. Taylor,
    6. Henry H. Chamberlin,
    7. Aury G. Coes,
    8. George R. Spurr.

City Clerk.

Samuel Smith.

Common Council.

Ward 1. Edward R. Fiske,
    John W. Howe,
    James S. Rogers.

    2. Samuel R. Heywood, *Pres't,*
    Henry Goddard,
    Thomas E. Tateum.

    3. Samuel McFadden,
    George F. Hewett,
    Eugene M. Moriarity.

    4. Patrick D. Conlin,
    Andrew Athy,
    John B. Cosgrove.

    5. John J. O'Gorman,
    John Cove,
    Patrick H. Carroll.

    6. George F. Wood,
    William H. Dexter,
    Nathan H. Chandler.

    7. Edwin Ames,
    Lucius J. Knowles,
    Calvin L. Hartshorn.

    8. Charles G. Parker,
    Enoch H. Towne,
    George Geer.

    Henry L. Shumway, *Clerk.*

1874.

Mayor.
EDWARD L. DAVIS.

Aldermen.
Ward 1. GEORGE S. HOPPIN,
2. LEWIS BARNARD,
3. WILLIAM H. JOURDAN,
4. SAMUEL D. HARDING,
5. RANSOM C. TAYLOR,
6. DORRANCE S. GODDARD,
7. AURY G. COES,
8. GEORGE R. SPURR.

City Clerk.
SAMUEL SMITH.

Common Council.
Ward 1. HAMILTON B. STAPLES,
ALFRED D. WARREN,
JAMES S. ROGERS.

2. GEORGE E. STEARNS,
HENRY GODDARD,
THOMAS E. TATEUM.

3. GEORGE F. HEWETT,
RICHARD BARKER,
EUGENE M. MORIARTY.

4. J. K. CHURCHILL,
ANDREW ATHY,
T. EDWARD MURRAY.

5. JOHN J. O'GORMAN,
JOHN COVE,
PATRICK H. CARROLL.

6. GEORGE F. WOOD,
WILLIAM H. DEXTER,
NATHAN H. CHANDLER.

7. CHARLES BELCHER,
CHARLES BALLARD,
CALVIN L. HARTSHORN.

8. CHARLES G. PARKER,
ENOCH H. TOWNE, *Pres't,*
GEORGE GEER.

HENRY L. SHUMWAY, *Clerk.*

1875.

Mayor.
CLARK JILLSON.

Aldermen.
Ward 1. HARRISON BLISS,
2. LEWIS BARNARD,
3. WILLIAM H. JOURDAN,
4. SAMUEL D. HARDING,
5. PETER J. TURNER,
6. DORRANCE S. GODDARD,
7. WARREN MCFARLAND,
8. GEORGE R. SPURR.

City Clerk.
SAMUEL SMITH.

Common Council.
Ward 1. HAMILTON B. STAPLES,
ALFRED D. WARREN,
THOMAS J. HASTINGS.

2. GEORGE E. STEARNS,
SAMUEL A. PORTER,
FRANCIS A. GASKILL.

3. GEORGE F. HEWETT,
RICHARD BARKER,
CORNELIUS O'SULLIVAN.

4. JAMES K. CHURCHILL,
ANDREW ATHY,
T. EDWARD MURRAY.

5. JOHN J. O'GORMAN,
THOMAS DOON,
WILLIAM KICKHAM.

6. WILLARD WARD,
LORING COES,
GILBERT J. RUGG.

7. CHARLES BELCHER,
CHARLES BALLARD, *Pres't,*
ALBERT A. LOVELL.

8. CHARLES G. PARKER,
GEORGE GEER,
OSCAR F. RAWSON.

HENRY L. SHUMWAY, *Clerk.*

1876.

Mayor.

CLARK JILLSON.

Aldermen.

Ward 1. HARRISON BLISS,
    2. JOHN M. WILLIAMS,
    3. WILLIAM H. JOURDAN,
    4. SAMUEL D. HARDING,
    5. STEPHEN SAWYER,
    6. MOWRY A. LAPHAM,
    7. WARREN MCFARLAND,
    8. SUMNER PRATT.

City Clerk.

SAMUEL SMITH.

Common Council.

Ward 1. THOMAS J. HASTINGS, *Pres't,*
    GEORGE E. BOYDEN,
    BENJAMIN WALKER.

    2. SAMUEL A. PORTER,
    FRANCIS A. GASKILL,
    ORRIN H. WESTON.

    3. CORNELIUS O'SULLIVAN,
    PAUL HENRY,
    JOHN B. O'LEARY.

    4. ANDREW ATHY,
    T. EDWARD MURRAY,
    JOHN J. O'GORMAN.

    5. WILLIAM KICKHAM,
    JOHN R. THAYER,
    WILLIAM O'CONNELL.

    6. LORING COES,
    GILBERT J. RUGG,
    ELLERY B. CRANE.

    7. ALBERT A. LOVELL,
    CALEB COLVIN,
    WILLIAM H. HEYWOOD.

    8. GEORGE GEER,
    OSCAR F. RAWSON,
    CHARLES BELCHER.

S. HAMILTON COE, *Clerk.*

1877.

Mayor.

CHARLES B. PRATT.

Aldermen.

Ward 1. WILLIAM DICKINSON,
    2. JOHN M. WILLIAMS,
    3. GEORGE P. KENDRICK,
    4. SAMUEL D. HARDING,
    5. STEPHEN SAWYER,
    6. MOWRY A. LAPHAM,
    7. WARREN MCFARLAND,
    8. SUMNER PRATT.

City Clerk.

ENOCH H. TOWNE.

Common Council.

Ward 1. GEORGE E. BOYDEN, *Pres't,*
    BENJAMIN WALKER,
    WILLIAM S. CLARK.

    2. ORRIN H. WESTON,
    SAMUEL A. PORTER,
    EDWIN H. HILL.

    3. PAUL HENRY,
    JOHN B. O'LEARY,
    ANDREW ATHY.

    4. JOHN J. O'GORMAN,
    PHILIP MOORE,
    FRANCIS PLUNKETT.

    5. JOHN R. THAYER,
    WILLIAM O'CONNELL,
    THOMAS MONAHAN.

    6. LORING COES,
    ELLERY B. CRANE,
    WILLIAM H. DEXTER.

    7. WILLIAM H. HEYWOOD,
    CALEB COLVIN,
    ALBERT A. LOVELL.

    8. CHARLES BELCHER,
    JOSEPH A. TITUS,
    THOMAS M. ROGERS.

S. HAMILTON COE, *Clerk.*

1878.

Mayor.

CHARLES B. PRATT.

Aldermen.

Ward 1. WILLIAM DICKINSON,
2. JOHN M. WILLIAMS,
3. GEORGE P. KENDRICK,
4. JOHN L. MURPHY,
5. STEPHEN SAWYER,
6. MOWRY A. LAPHAM,
7. WARREN McFARLAND,
8. HENRY A. MARSH.

City Clerk.

ENOCH H. TOWNE.

Common Council.

Ward 1. GEORGE E. BOYDEN, *Pres't,*
F. P. STOWELL,
WILLIAM S. CLARK.

2. OLIVER P. SHATTUCK,
SAMUEL A. PORTER,
EDWIN H. HILL.

3. PAUL HENRY,
JAMES B. McMAHON,
ANDREW ATHY.

4. JOHN J. O'GORMAN,
PHILIP MOORE,
FRANCIS PLUNKETT.

5. WILLIAM O'CONNELL,
JOHN R. THAYER,
THOMAS MONAHAN.

6. ELLERY B. CRANE,
LORING COES,
WILLIAM H. DEXTER.

7. WILLIAM H. HEYWOOD,
JAMES A. NORCROSS,
ALBERT A. LOVELL.

8. FRANK E. LANCASTER,
JOSEPH A. TITUS,
THOMAS M. ROGERS.

S. HAMILTON COE, *Clerk.*

1879.

Mayor.

CHARLES B. PRATT.

Aldermen.

Ward 1. SENECA M. RICHARDSON,
2. JOHN M. WILLIAMS,
3. GEORGE P. KENDRICK,
4. JOHN L. MURPHY,
5. STEPHEN SAWYER,
6. MOWRY A. LAPHAM,
7. FRANK H. KELLEY,
8. HENRY A. MARSH.

City Clerk.

ENOCH H. TOWNE.

Common Council.

Ward 1. WILLIAM S. CLARK,
GEORGE E. BOYDEN, *Pres't,*
FRANCIS P. STOWELL.

2. GEORGE A. BARNARD,
SAMUEL A. PORTER,
OLIVER P. SHATTUCK.

3. ANDREW ATHY,
PAUL HENRY,
JAMES B. McMAHON.

4. FRANCIS PLUNKETT,
JOHN J. WHITE,
JOHN J. O'GORMAN.

5. PATRICK J. QUINN,
WILLIAM O'CONNELL,
JOHN R. THAYER.

6. LORING COES,
SAMUEL MAWHINNEY,
ELLERY B. CRANE.

7. HIRAM FOBES,
WILLIAM H. HEYWOOD,
JAMES A. NORCROSS.

8. THOMAS TALBOT,
FREDERICK W. WARD,
FRANK E. LANCASTER.

S. HAMILTON COE, *Clerk.*

1880.

Mayor.

FRANK H. KELLEY.

Aldermen.

Ward 1. SENECA M. RICHARDSON,
2. CHARLES G. REED,
3. GEORGE P. KENDRICK,
4. CHARLES C. HOUGHTON,
5. STEPHEN SAWYER,
6. MOWRY A. LAPHAM,
7. GEORGE F. HEWETT,
8. HENRY A. MARSH.

City Clerk.

ENOCH H. TOWNE.

Common Council.

Ward 1. J. LEWIS ELLSWORTH,
ALBERT S. BROWN,
WILLIAM S. CLARK.

2. OLIVER P. SHATTUCK, *Pres't.*
GEORGE A. BARNARD,
SAMUEL A. PORTER.

3. DANIEL J. SAVAGE,
JAMES B. McMAHON,
ANDREW ATHY.

4. JAMES J. TIERNEY,
FRANCIS PLUNKETT,
JOHN J. WHITE.

5. THOMAS DANIELS,
BENJAMIN BOOTH,
PATRICK J. QUINN.

6. SAMUEL C. ANDREWS,
LORING COES,
SAMUEL MAWHINNEY.

7. GEORGE E. BATCHELDER,
GRANVILLE A. LONGLEY,
HIRAM FOBES.

8. FRANK E. LANCASTER,
THOMAS TALBOT,
FREDERICK W. WARD.

S. HAMILTON COE, *Clerk.*

Joint Rules and Orders

CITY COUNCIL.

———

SECT. I. At the commencement of the muni- What committees shall be appointed at the commencement of the municipal year. cipal year, the following joint standing committees shall be chosen or appointed by their respective boards :—

A committee on finance.

A committee on claims.

A committee on printing.

A committee on highways and sidewalks.

A committee on water.

A committee on fire department.

A committee on lighting streets.

A committee on military affairs.

A committee on education.

A committee on charities.

A committee on ordinances.

A committee on sewers.

A committee on public buildings.

A committee to assign the mayor's inaugural address, and all unfinished business of the previous

How committees
shall be consti-
tuted.

year.   Each of the above committees shall consist of two aldermen and three members of the common council, except when it may be otherwise ordered.

How joint com-
mittees shall be
constituted.

SECT. 2.   In all joint committees, the number of members from the common council shall be one greater than the number from the board of aldermen.

Who shall be }
chairman.

SECT. 3.   The mayor shall be, *ex-officio*, chairman of any joint committee of which he is a member ; and of other joint committees, the first named member of the board of aldermen ; and in case of his resignation or absence, the next named member of

Absence of
chairman.

the same board ; and afterwards, the member of the common council first in order, shall call the meetings of the committee, and act as chairman.

Non-concur-
rence.

SECT. 4.   When either board shall not concur with the other in any ordinance, order or resolution, sent from such other, notice of such non-concurrence shall forthwith be given.

Committees of
conference.

SECT. 5.   In every case of disagreement on any matter requiring the joint action of the two boards, if either board shall request a conference, and appoint a committee for that purpose, the other board shall appoint a committee to confer with them ; each committee shall consist of three members on the part of each board representing its vote. Said com- mittees shall meet at a time appointed by the chairman of the committee on the part of the board requesting the conference, and state to each other the reasons of their respective boards, for or against the proposed action, and report at the same or at the next regular meeting; and their report, if agreed to by a majority of each committee, shall be first acted on by the board asking the conference, and may be either accepted or rejected.

SECT. 6. Each board shall transmit to the other all papers on which any ordinance, joint order or resolution shall be founded, and all papers on their passage between the two boards, shall be under the signatures of their respective clerks or presiding officers.

SECT. 7. Either board may propose to the other, for its concurrence, a time to which both shall adjourn, which subject shall have precedence over other business; and when the time has been fixed, either board may adjourn, unless it is otherwise requested, and the reasons therefor are given by the board making the request.

SECT. 8. When any matter is referred to a joint committee, the city clerk shall furnish the clerk of

City clerk shall furnish copy of votes, &c. such committee with a copy or the original, of all votes or papers pertaining to the subject matter referred, within forty-eight hours. The reports of all committees, signed by a majority of the members thereof, may be made to either board, except in case of committees of conference.

What reports shall be received. SECT. 9. No committee shall act by separate consultation, and no reports, except minority reports, shall be received, unless they shall have been agreed to in committee actually assembled, and no report shall be received recommending the expenditure of money, unless it shall contain a careful estimate of the amount required.

Reports to be made within four weeks. SECT. 10. It shall be the duty of every joint committee, to whom any subject shall be specially referred, unless otherwise ordered, to report thereon, within four weeks, or ask for further time.

Contracts. SECT. 11. No committee shall enter into any contract with any of its members, nor purchase or authorize the purchase of any articles of any such member.

Approval of bills. SECT. 12. No chairman of any committee shall audit or approve any bill or account against the city for any supplies or services, unless ordered so to do

by vote of the committee at a meeting regularly
called, which vote shall be certified by its clerk.

SECT. 13. Joint standing committees shall cause Records.
records to be kept of their proceedings, in books
provided by the city for that purpose.

SECT. 14. All reports and other papers submitted Reports.
to the city council, shall be written in a fair hand,
and the clerks of the boards, respectively, shall make
copies of any papers to be reported by committees,
at the request of the respective chairmen thereof.

SECT. 15. No business shall be transacted by the Business in con-
ventions.
city council in convention, except such as shall have
been previously agreed on, unless by unanimous
consent.

SECT. 16. Every joint resolution shall have as Manner of passing Joint Reso-
many readings in each board as the rules of that lutions.
board require, after which the question shall be, on
passing the same, and when the same shall have
been passed, it shall be sent to the other board for
concurrence, and when such resolution shall have so
passed in each board, the same shall be enrolled by
the clerk of the common council, and examined by
a committee of that board; and, on being found by
said committee to be correctly enrolled, without fur-

ther reading or question shall be signed by the president of the common council, and sent to the other board, where a like examination shall be made by a committee of that board, and, if found correctly enrolled, the same shall be signed by the mayor.

Manner of passing ordinances.

SECT. 17. Every ordinance shall have as many readings in each board as the rules of that board require, after which the question shall be on passing the same to be enrolled, and when the same shall have passed to be enrolled, it shall be sent to the other board for concurrence; and when such ordinance shall have so passed to be enrolled in each board the same shall be enrolled by the clerk of the common council, and examined by a committee of that board, and, on being found by said committee to be correctly enrolled, the same shall be reported to the council, when the question shall be on passing the same to be ordained, and when said ordinance shall have so passed to be ordained, it shall be signed by the president of the common council, and sent to the other board, where a like examination shall be made by a committee of that board, and, if found correctly enrolled, the same shall be reported to the board, and the question shall be on passing the same to be ordained; and when the same shall have passed to be ordained, it shall be signed by the mayor.

SECT. 18. After the annual appropriations shall have been made, no subsequent expenditure shall be authorized for any object, unless provision for the same shall be made by a specific transfer from some of the appropriations contained in the annual order, or by expressly creating therefor a city debt; but no such debt shall be created, unless the order authorizing the same, pass by the affirmative votes of two-thirds of the whole number of each branch of the city council, voting by yeas and nays.

Appropriations after the annual appropriations.

SECT. 19. No expenditure shall be made for the providing of armories for the use of military companies, for the celebration of holidays, and for other purposes of a public nature, unless the order authorizing said expenditure shall be adopted by a vote of two-thirds of the members of each branch of the city council present, and voting by yeas and nays.

Extra appropriations.

SECT. 20. The city clerk shall be clerk of the city council in convention and also clerk of all joint committees where no other provision is made.

City clerk to be clerk of city council when in convention.

SECT. 21. All salaried officers chosen by the city council shall be elected by ballot and in all elections by ballot, blanks shall be reported but not counted as votes.

Elections.

Parliamentary
practice.

SECT. 22.   When the two branches are in convention, and there occurs any difference of opinion in regard to modes of proceeding not otherwise provided for, the city council shall be governed by parliamentary practice as set forth in "Cushing's Manual of the Law and Practice of Legislative Assemblies."

Rules and Orders

BOARD OF ALDERMEN.

SECTION 1. The order of business shall be as follows :

First. The mayor shall call the board to order, Order of business. and if a quorum be present, shall cause the roll to be called, and the names of the absentees recorded.

Second. The journal of the previous meeting shall be read.

Third. Petitions, reports and other papers requiring the action of the common council shall be called for, and be disposed of by reference or otherwise.

Fourth. The orders of the day shall be taken up — meaning by the orders of the day, the business remaining unfinished at the previous meeting, and such communications as may have been subsequently sent up from the common council.

Fifth. New business may be introduced by any member of the board.

Sixth. Such nominations, appointments and elections as may be in order, shall be considered and disposed of.   .

Manner of passing ordinances. SECT. 2. Every ordinance shall pass through the following stages before it shall be considered as having received the final action of this board, viz: first reading, second reading, passage to be enrolled, passage to be ordained; and every joint resolution shall have two several readings, before the question shall be taken on its final passage.

How resolves and orders may be disposed of. SECT. 3. A resolve, an order for appropriating money, or an ordinance, may be rejected at either stage in its progress, but may not pass through all its stages in one day except by general consent.

Committees. SECT. 4. Standing committees shall be appointed on assessments for sewers; on assessments for street betterments; on enrollment; on bills in the second reading, and on elections and returns.

Interruptions. SECT. 5. No member shall be interrupted while speaking, but by a call to order, or for a correction of a mistake, nor shall there be any conversation ' among the members while a paper is being read, or a question stated from the chair.

SECT. 6. The foregoing rules, and order of business, shall be observed in all cases, unless suspended for a specific purpose by a vote of two-thirds of the members present.

Suspension of rules.

SECT. 7. All committees shall be appointed and announced by the mayor, unless the board shall determine otherwise.

Appointment of committees.

Rules and Orders

OF THE

COMMON COUNCIL.

RIGHTS AND DUTIES OF THE PRESIDENT.

Calling to order, calling the roll, and reading minutes.

SECTION 1. The president shall take the chair at the hour apppointed for the meeting, call the members to order, and, if a quorum be present, cause the roll to be called, and the names of the absentees recorded. He shall then call for the reading of the minutes of the preceding meeting, and proceed to business.

Questions of order and appeals.

SECT. 2. He shall preserve order and decorum, may speak to points of order in preference to other members, and shall decide all such questions, subject to an appeal to the council by motion regularly seconded; and no other business shall be in order till the question on the appeal shall have been decided. He shall also nominate all committees

Nomination of committees.

not elected by ballot, unless the council shall determine otherwise.

SECT. 3. He shall arisé to address the council, to state facts, or to put a question, but may read sitting. *President may read, sitting*

SECT. 4. When a question is under debate, the president shall receive no motion but to adjourn, to lay on the table, for the previous question, to postpone to a certain day, to commit, to amend, or to postpone indefinitely; which several motions shall have precedence in the order in which they are arranged. He shall declare all votes, but if a vote be doubted he shall order a return of the number voting in the affirmative and in the negative without any further debate. *Order of precedence. Doubted votes.*

SECT. 5. He may call any member to the chair for a period of time not extending beyond an adjournment; and when out of the chair, the president may participate in any debate; but shall not resume the chair while the same question is pending; and on going into a committee of the whole, he shall appoint the chairman. *President may take part in debate. Committee of the whole.*

SECT. 6. Questions shall be propounded in the order in which they are moved; unless the subsequent motion be previous in its nature: except that in naming sums and fixing times, the largest sum and the longest time shall be first put. *Order of propounding questions.*

Disposition of motions.

SECT. 7.   After a motion is stated by the president, it shall be disposed of by a vote of the council, unless withdrawn by the mover before an amendment or decision.

Motions to adjourn, and to lay on table.

SECT. 8.   A motion to adjourn shall always be in order; that, and the motion to lay on the table, shall be decided without debate.

Previous question.

SECT. 9.   The previous question shall be put in this form: "Shall the main question be now put?" It only shall be admitted when demanded by a majority of the members present; and, until it is decided, shall preclude all amendment and debate of the main question, and after the adoption of the previous question, the sense of the council shall forthwith be taken upon amendments reported by a committee, upon all pending amendments, and then upon the main question.

Yeas and nays.

SECT. 10.   On all questions and motions whatsoever, the president shall take the sense of the council by yeas and nays, provided one fifth of the members present shall so require.

When two or more members rise at the same time.

SECT. 11.   When two or more members rise at the same time, the president shall name the member who is to speak first.

RIGHTS AND DUTIES OF MEMBERS.

SECT. 12. In the absence of the president, the *President pro- tempore.* member present whose election is of the earliest date shall call the council to order, and preside until a president *pro tempore* shall be chosen 'by ballot; and if an election is not effected on the first trial, on a second ballot a plurality of votes shall elect. When any member is about to speak in the *Manner of speaking.* council, he shall rise in his place and respectfully address the presiding officer, confining himself to the question under debate, and avoiding personalities.

SECT. 13. No member shall be mentioned in the *Personalities.* debate by his name, but may be described by the place he occupies, or such other designation as may be intelligible and respectful.

SECT. 14. No member speaking shall be inter- *Interruptions.* rupted by another, but by a call to order or to correct a mistake.

SECT. 15. No person shall speak more than *Number of times a member may* once on a question, to the prevention of any other *speak on the same ques-* who has not spoken and is desirous to speak; nor *tion.* more than twice without the consent of the board; and all questions relating to priority of business, shall be taken without debate.

Members to remain seated.

SECT. 16. When the president or any other member is speaking, no one shall stand up, or pass unnecessarily before the person speaking.

Reducing motions to writing.

SECT. 17. Every motion shall be reduced to writing if the president or any member require it.

Reconsideration.

SECT. 18. A motion to reconsider a vote shall only be in order at the same or the meeting next

Postponement of motions to reconsider.

succeeding that at which the vote was passed. If a motion is made to reconsider a vote at the same meeting at which it is passed, and it is moved to postpone its consideration until the next meeting, such motion to postpone shall require for its adoption the affirmative vote of but one-fourth of the

Proviso.

members ' voting; and, *provided further*, that no action of the council upon a motion to reconsider a vote, upon an incidental or subsidiary question, shall remove the main subject under consideration, from

A motion to reconsider cannot be reconsidered.

before it. When a motion for reconsideration is decided, that decision shall not be reconsidered.

Motion to postpone not debatable.

The motion to " postpone until the next meeting " the consideration of a motion to reconsider a vote, shall not be debatable, and shall not be in order, on and after the last Monday in December.

All members present shall vote.

SECT. 19. Every member who shall be in the council when a question is put, shall give his vote, unless the council for special reasons excuse him, or unless his private interest is involved therein.

SECT. 20. No motion or proposition on a subject Amendments. different from that under consideration, shall be admitted under color of an amendment.

SECT. 21. All reports may be committed or Committing and re-committed at the pleasure of the council. And re-committing. when a motion is made to refer a subject, and When different different committees are proposed, the question committees are shall be taken in the order following : proposed.

A standing committee of the council.

A select committee of the council.

A joint standing committee.

A joint select committee.

SECT. 22. All questions shall be divided when Divisions of the sense will admit of it, if called for by any questions. member of the council.

SECT. 23. No rule or standing order of the Rules may be council shall be suspended, unless three-fourths of suspended. the members present consent thereto ; nor shall any rule or order be repealed or amended, without one day's notice being given of the motion therefor, Repeal of rules nor unless a majority of the whole council concur and orders. therein.

Serving on
committees.

SECT. 24.   No member shall be obliged to serve on more that two committees at the same time, nor be chairman of more than one nor on any committee having in charge matter touching his individual interest.

Parliamentary
Law.

SECT. 25.   All differences of opinion in regard to points of order or modes of proceeding not otherwise provided for, shall be governed by Parliamentary practice, as set forth in Cushing's "Law and Practice of Legislative Assembles."

COMMUNICATIONS, COMMITTEES, REPORTS, RESOLUTIONS, ETC.

Communications.

SECT. 26.   All papers addressed to the council shall be presented by the president, or by a member in his place, and shall be read by the president, clerk, or such other person as the president may request, and shall be taken up in the order in which they were presented, unless when the council shall otherwise direct.

Committees.

SECT. 27.   Standing committees shall be appointed on bills in the second reading, on enrollment, and on elections and returns.

Their time of
sitting.

SECT. 28.   No committee shall sit during the sitting of the council, without special leave, except the committee on the second reading of bills and ordinances, and the committee on enrollment.

SECT. 29.   The rules' of proceeding in the council Rules to apply to committee of the whole. shall be observed in the committee of the whole, so far as they may be applicable, except the rule limiting the times of speaking.

SECT. 30.   When a committee is nominated by Chairmen of committees. the chair, the first person named shall be the chairman.   In elections of committees by ballot, when the chairman is not specially chosen, the person having the highest number of votes shall act as chairman, and in case of an equality of votes between two or more members of a committee, the members thereof shall choose a chairman.

SECT. 31.   All ordinances, orders and resolutions, Ordinances, etc., shall have two readings. shall have two several readings before they shall be finally passed by the council.

SECT. 32.   All ordinances, before being read a Ordinances, how passed. second time, shall be referred to the committee on the second reading of bills and ordinances ; and after being reported upon by said committee, shall be again read, after which second reading the question shall be on passing the same to be enrolled.   An ordinance shall not pass through all its stages in one day.

Ordinances, &c., authorizing expenditure or loans, or imposing penalties.

SECT. 33. All ordinances, orders or resolutions, imposing penalties or authorizing the expenditure of money, whether the same may have been appropriated or not, and all orders or resolutions authorizing a loan, shall have but one reading on the same day,

Proviso.

provided, however, that nothing herein contained shall prevent the passage of an order at any meeting of the council, to authorize the printing of any documents relating to the affairs of the city.

Seats.

SECT. 34. The seats of the common council shall be numbered, and determined by lot, and no member shall change his seat, but by permission of the president.

Of how many committees shall consist.

SECT. 35. All committees of the council shall consist of three members, unless a different number be specially ordered. And no report shall be received from any committee, unless actually assembled; and all reports shall be in writing.

Reports.

Reports to be made within four weeks.

SECT. 36. It shall be the duty of every committee of the council to whom any subject may be specially referred, to report thereon within four weeks, or ask further time.

ELECTIONS.

Officers, how elected.

SECT. 37. All salaried officers shall be chosen by ballot; blanks shall be reported, but not counted as votes.

DUTIES OF CLERK, ETC.

SECT. 38.   The clerk shall keep brief minutes of the votes and proceedings of the council, entering thereon all accepted resolutions ; shall notice reports and memorials, and other papers submitted to the board, only by their titles, or a brief description of their purport.   When the yeas and nays are taken, the clerk shall call the names of all the members except the president, in alphabetical order. *Duties of clerk.*

SECT. 39.   The clerk of the common council shall keep the record of committees who may require that service ; and on the appointment of every standing committee, a book for record shall be provided by its chairman or by said clerk ; and the clerk shall have the custody of all the minutes by him kept, and the records of the several committees shall be open to the inspection of the members of the city council. *Shall have custody of records.*

SECT. 40.   The clerk shall notify, in writing, the chairmen of all committees of the council, of the appointment of such committees. *Shall notify chairmen of committees of appointments.*

CITY OFFICERS.

Elected by the citizens by ballot in wards on the Tuesday next following the second Monday of December, annually:

MAYOR, for the municipal year next following his election, - -	8
ALDERMEN, for two years from the first Monday of January next following their election, - - - - -	8
COMMON COUNCILMEN, for two years from the first Monday of January next following their election, - - - -	8
ASSISTANT ASSESSORS, for the municipal year next following their election, - - - - - - - -	23
WARDENS, for the municipal year next following their election, -	5
INSPECTORS OF ELECTIONS, for the municipal year next following their election, - - - - - - -	5
WARD CLERKS, for the municipal year next following their election,	5
SCHOOL COMMITTEE, for three years, from the first Monday of January following their election, - - - -	24

Elected by City Council in Convention, in January:

AUDITOR, for one year, - - - - - -	108
COMMISSIONER OF HIGHWAYS, for one year, - - - -	108
COMMISSIONER OF PUBLIC GROUNDS, &c., for three years, - -	108
TREASURER AND COLLECTOR OF TAXES, for one year, - -	108
CITY ENGINEER, for one year, - - - - -	108
CITY CLERK, for one year, - - - - - -	108
COMMISSIONER OF HOPE CEMETERY, for five years, - - -	109
MESSENGER, for one year, - - - - - -	108
SOLICITOR, for one year, - - - - - -	108
WATER COMMISSIONER, for one year, - - - - .	108
WATER REGISTRAR, for one year, - - - - -	108
SUPERINTENDENT OF PUBLIC BUILDINGS, for one year, - -	109
SUPERINTENDENT OF SEWERS, for one year, - - - -	109

COMMISSIONER OF THE JAQUES FUND AND OTHER FUNDS OF THE
    CITY HOSPITAL, for three years,   -   -   -   -   109

In February or March:

ASSESSOR OF TAXES, for three years from his election,   -   -   109

In December:

CHIEF ENGINEER OF THE FIRE DEPARTMENT, for one year from
    the first Monday in January next ensuing,   -   -   45, 109
FOUR ASSISTANT ENGINEERS OF THE FIRE DEPARTMENT, for one
    year from the first Monday in January next ensuing,   -   45, 109
TWO DIRECTORS OF FREE PUBLIC LIBRARY, for six years, from the
    first day of January next ensuing,   -   -   -   -   109
TWO OVERSEERS OF THE POOR, for three years from the third
    Monday in January next ensuing,—no more than one member
    of the board, shall be eligible from any one ward,— -   - 22, 109

Elected by concurrent vote in January:

FOUR TRUSTEES OF THE CITY HOSPITAL,   -   -   -   109
    One member of the board of aldermen, two members of the
    common council, for one year, one citizen at large, for four
    years,   -   -   -   -   -   -   -   106

In February:

THREE FENCE VIEWERS, for one year,   -   -   -   -   109
FIELD DRIVERS, for one year,   -   -   -   -   -   109
POUND KEEPER, for one year, -   -   -   -   -   109
SURVEYORS OF LUMBER, for one year,   -   -   -   -   106

Elected by concurrent vote biennially in February or March:

[1] ONE REGISTRAR OF VOTERS (who shall be Clerk of the Board), for
    two years, from his election,   -   -   -   -   -   109

Elected by concurrent vote in December:

ONE COMMISSIONER OF THE SINKING FUNDS, for three years, from
    the first Monday of January next ensuing,   -   -   -   110

---

[1] The present term began March 24, 1879.

Appointed by the Mayor and Aldermen, in January:

[1] CITY PHYSICIAN, for three years, from his appointment, -   -   110
ONE MEMBER OF THE BOARD OF HEALTH, for two years from the
    first Monday in February next succeeding,   -   -   - 110
CITY MARSHAL, for one year, -   -   -   -   -   - 111

TWO ASSISTANT MARSHALS, for one year, -   -   -   - 111
CAPTAIN OF NIGHT POLICE, for one year, -   -   -   - 111
POLICEMEN, for one year,   -   -   -   -   -   - 111
CONSTABLES, for one year,   -   -   -   -   -   - 111

In March :

SEALER OF WEIGHTS AND MEASURES, for one year,   -   - 110
MEASURERS OF WOOD, BARK, &C., for one year,   -   -   - 110
WEIGHERS OF HAY AND OTHER ARTICLES, -   -   -   - 110
FUNERAL UNDERTAKERS, for one year,   -   -   -   - 110
INSPECTOR OF MILK, for one year, -   -   -   -   - 110
WEIGHERS OF COAL, for one year, (St. 1870, ch. 205, sec. 2).
INSPECTOR OF VINEGAR, for one year, (St. 1880, ch. 113).
INSPECTOR OF PETROLEUM, &C., for one year,   -   -   - 169

In October :

AN INSPECTOR OF ELECTIONS FOR EACH WARD, for three years
    from the first day of November then next succeeding,   - 110

Elected by the Common Council :

PRESIDENT, -   -   -   -   -   -   -   - . 10
CLERK, -   -   -   -   -   -   -   -   - 10

Elected by the School Committee :

SUPERINTENDENT OF SCHOOLS,   -   -   -   -   - 179
TRUANT OFFICERS, (St. 1873, ch. 262, sec. 2),

---

[1] The present term began March 24, 1879.

INDEX.

27

CITY HOSPITAL.—*Continued.*
   vacancies, 118.
   removal of, 111.
   to organize, 119.
   quorum, 119.
   how to invest funds, 119.
   pay surplus to city treasurer, 119.
   may sell real estate, 120.
   to report, 121.
   general bequests income only to be used, 121.
   bonds, oaths, &c., 234.
CITY MARSHAL, See *Police.*
   to be appointed by mayor and aldermen, 12.
   may be removed by mayor and aldermen, 13.
   may be required to give bond, 13, 234.
   all officers receiving, &c., money, shall give bond, 16.
   to have the powers and duties of constables, 12.
   to be *ex officio*, a member of the board of the overseers of the poor, 22.
   shall have charge of all constables, assistant marshals, and police-officers, 173.
   shall report to mayor and aldermen any violation of duty, 173.
   shall pass through streets, lanes, &c., observe nuisances and remove them, 173.
   to report defects in streets, roads or highways, to commissioner of highways, 173.
   shall prosecute all offenders, 173.
   shall enforce all laws and ordinances, 173.
   shall receive complaints for violation of ordinances, 173.
   when complaint of disturbance by dogs is made, 127.
   power over hoisting apparatus, 208.
   who may direct, 174.
   duties relating to health, 174.
   shall keep a descriptive list of all persons arrested, 175.
   to keep a record of his doings, 175.
   mayor and aldermen, may inspect the record, 175.

CITY PROPERTY, city council to have management of, 35.
    may purchase, 35.
CITY SEAL, ordinance establishing, 181.
    city clerk shall be keeper of, 112.
    deeds, &c., to be sealed with, 126.
    licenses to be sealed with, 234.
CITY SOLICITOR, election, compensation, and removal of,
    15, 108, 111.
    tenure of office, 15, 111.
    duties of, 193.
    shall report to city council annually, 194.
CITY OF WORCESTER, charter of, 3.
    city council since 1848, 248.
CLERICAL LABOR, not to be employed without the concur-
    rence of the finance committee, 133.
CLERK. See *City Clerk, &c.*
COACHES. See *Hackney and other Carriages.*
COAL, inspection of, &c., may be regulated, 27.
    in quantities of over five hundred pounds, to be weighed, 198.
    not to remain in streets, 202, 204, 209.
COASTING regulated, 205.
COLLECTOR OF TAXES. See *Treasurer.*
COMMISSIONER OF HIGHWAYS, election of, 15, 108.
    compensation, term of office, and removal of, 15, 111.
    shall superintend the streets, &c., 113.
    shall attend to grading, repairs, &c., 113.
    remove obstructions, 113.
    may order obstructions removed, 204.
    make certain contracts, 113.
    have charge of certain property, 113.
    break out roads after snow storms, 113.
    guard unsafe places, 113.
    make estimates of proposed alterations, &c., 114.
    to keep accounts and report to auditor, 115.
    to repair roofs, &c., 115.
    grade, &c., sidewalks, 186.
    to keep an account of the expense and report to auditor,
    186.
    to make repairs of sidewalks, 187.

ELECTION AND APPOINTMENT, of officers, ordinance
    regulating, 108.
    list of officers, with the time and manner of election or ap-
        pointment, 286.
    elections to be in wards, &c., 27.
    for details, see their respective titles.
    of school committee may be held on separate day, 24, note 1.
    statute provisions, 27, note.
    see *Registrars of Voters, Warrants. &c.*
ELM PARK, lying on seats or playing games, 179.
ENGINE COMPANIES. See *Fire Department.*
ENGINEER. See *City Engineer.*
ENGINEERS, of fire department. See *Fire Department.*
ENGINE MEN. See *Fire Department.*
EXECUTIVE POWER vested in mayor and aldermen, 12.
EXPENDITURES, not to exceed appropriations, 16. See *Aud-*
    itor, Finance Committee, &c.
EXPLOSIVES, regulated, 149, 169.
FARE, rate of, how established, 233.
FAST DRIVING, prohibited, 206.
FEES, rate of, how established, 233.
FEMALES. See *Women.*
FENCES, not to be injured in streets, 211.
    not to be injured around public grounds, 178.
    not to be built into streets, 206, 208.
    horses, &c., not to be tied to, 208.
    adjoining public grounds, &c., 206.
    bills, &c., not to be posted on, 205.
FENCE VIEWERS, election of, 109.
    compensation and removal of, 111.
    records to be open for inspection, 131.
FIELD DRIVERS, election of, 109.
    compensation and removal of, 111.
FIGHTING OF BIRDS, prohibited, 211.
FILTH, not to be placed in any public grounds, 178.
FINAL JUDGMENTS, may be paid without order of finance
    committee, 132.
    amount to be reported by auditor to assessors, 102.

FINANCE. See *Auditor, Accounts, Finance Committee, City Hospital, Treasurer.*

FINANCE COMMITTEE, election of, 131.

of whom to consist, 131.

members, *ex-officio,* 131.

auditor to be clerk of, 100.

meetings to be held monthly, at least, 131.

committee to consider and report on finances, 131.

to negotiate loans, 132.

bills to be examined by, after auditor's certificate, 132.

money not to be paid without order of committee, 132.

clerical labor, 133.

books and accounts, to be kept under the direction of the committee, 132.

bills and accounts, to be certified as directed by the committee, 133.

auditor's books to be kept as the committee direct, 99.

doubtful bills to be presented to committee by auditor, 100.

may direct auditor, 101.

may require board of health to present estimates, 159.

may direct the treasurer, 220.

to examine, &c., the accounts of the treasurer, 133.

to examine notes and other securities of the city and report fully to the city council, 133.

FINANCIAL YEAR, 219.

FINES AND FORFEITURES, for violation of ordinances, to be paid to the city, 29.

FIRE, buildings may be demolished to prevent the spreading of, 135.

inspection and use of buildings, 218.

See *Fire Department. Fire Limits.*

FIREARMS, not to be discharged, 133.

FIRE COMPANIES. See *Fire Department.*

FIRE DEPARTMENT. See *Worcester Protective Department.*

charter provisions concerning, 15, 27.

authority to establish the department, 85.

ordinance establishing, 134.

city council shall provide for appointments and removals, 85.

FIRE DEPARTMENT.—*Continued.*

    fix qualifications and period of service, 85.

    office and duty, 85.

    compensation, 85, 141.

    regulate conduct and management of fires, 85.

    may act by agents, &c., 86.

    Worcester protective department, not to interfere with, 88.

    seniority, rank, &c., to be determined by the mayor and aldermen, 138.

    supplies, how drawn, 138.

    Chief Engineer. Election of, 109.

    vacancy, compensation and removal, 111, 140.

    dangerous buildings, shavings, &c., 135, 136.

    to report annually, 136.

    may suspend officers and members, 137.

    when they are not reinstated, 137.

    may allow water to be taken from reservoirs, 141.

    may inspect companies, 137.

    may direct engineers to go out of the city to a fire, 136.

    he shall have the sole command at fires, 137.

    with other engineers may order buildings demolished, 135.

    to take care of property used by the department, 137.

    to keep records, &c., 137.

    may direct the clerk of the board of engineers, 138.

    to inspect petroleum, &c., 170.

ASSISTANT ENGINEERS, four to be elected, 109.

    vacancies, removal, compensation, 111.

    to command in the absence of the chief, 138.

    to inspect petroleum, &c., 170.

ENGINEERS, BOARD OF, to organize, 134.

    names of persons suspended by chief, to be reported to, 137.

    may remove members or depose from office, 140.

    to transmit reasons, &c., to the aldermen, 141.

    officers removed to be re-instated only by vote, &c., 141.

    may prescribe badges and uniforms, 136.

    may inspect records of foremen, 140.

    who may direct clerk, 138.

    duties of clerk, 138.

GAS LIGHT CO.—*Continued.*
 extension of pipes by direction of city council, 81
 no shares issued less than par, 79, 82.
 par value, 79, note 3.
 may open ground to lay pipes, with the consent of the mayor
  and aldermen, 79, 82.
 mayor and aldermen may control acts affecting health, &c.
  80, 83.
 charges for gas, not to exceed certain cities, 81.
GATES, not to swing over sidewalks, &c., 211.
GENERAL MEETINGS, of citizens, may be held, 28.
 to be called, on request of fifty voters, 28.
 warrants for, to be issued by the mayor and aldermen, 6.
 form, service, &c., to be prescribed by the city council, 6.
 ordinance regulating, 225.
GOATS, may be removed from the city, 162.
 keeping of may be prohibited, 162.
 not to go at large, 207.
GOODS, not to obstruct streets, 202.
GOVERNMENT OF THE CITY, from 1848 to 1880, inclusive, 248.
GRAZING ANIMALS, not allowed on commons, 178.
GUIDE POSTS, not to be injured, 211.
GUN COTTON, keeping of, to be regulated, 148, 149.
GUNPOWDER, how to be kept, 149.
 using, 148.
GUTTERS. See *Sidewalks.*
 from roofs, not to discharge water on streets, sidewalks,
  &c., 214.
 alteration of, 115.
HACKNEY AND OTHER CARRIAGES, to be licensed,
  152, 155.
 persons licensed to give bond, 153.
 expiration and transfer of licenses, 156.
 fee for licenses, 155.
 illegal fare, 154, 157.
 persons licensed, shall not unreasonably refuse to carry
  passengers, at established rates, 154.

HERMITAGE BROOK, power over, 69.
HIGHWAYS. See *Commissioner of, and Streets*.
HOGS. See *Swine*.
HOISTING MERCHANDISE, over streets, 208.
HOOK AND LADDER COMPANIES. See *Fire Department*.
HOOK AND LADDER MEN. See *Fire Department*.
HOOPS, not to be rolled in streets, 210.
HOPE CEMETERY. See *Commissioners of*.
HORNS, not to be blown, 205.
HORSES, fast driving of, prohibited, 206.
    not allowed on sidewalks, 206.
    not to go at large in streets, 207.
    not to go upon any public common, 178.
    not to stand in street, without being tied, 207.
    not to be tied to lamp posts, trees, &c., 208.
    not to be stopped upon any footwalk, 207.
    frightening horses forbidden, 215.
    see *Hackney Carriages, and Streets*.
HOSEMEN. See *Fire Department*.
HOSPITAL. See *City Hospital*.
HOUSE OFFAL. See *Health*.
HOUSES. See *Buildings*.
ICE, removal of, from sidewalks and roofs, 213.
IMPURE WATER, not to flow on streets, &c., 211.
INCOMPATIBILITY OF OFFICES, 14.
    overseers of the poor, 22.
    registrars of voters, 36.
    sinking fund commissioners, 188.
INCUMBRANCES. See *Streets*.
INDECENT LANGUAGE, in streets, &c., 214.
    by hackmen, &c.. prohibited, 153.
INDENTURES, execution of, 126.
INFECTIOUS DISEASES. See *Health*.
INOCULATION. See *Vaccination of Scholars*.
INSPECTION OF BUILDINGS. See *Superintendent of Public Buildings*.

LICENSES.—*Continued.*

   to be pawnbroker, 167.

   to obstruct streets, 202.

   to dig up streets, 202.

   to move, &c., buildings in streets, &c., 203.

   to move wooden buildings, 147.

   to enlarge, &c., wooden buildings, 147.

   to build mills, &c., outside of fire limits, 148.

   to erect or remove posts, 204.

   to blast rocks, &c., 204.

   to water streets, 205.

   stands for hay, &c., 196.

   to sell kerosene, petroleum, &c., 169.

   to lay drains, 184.

   to keep stables for over four horses, 195,

   stables within one hundred feet of a church, &c., 195.

   to maintain a bulletin board, 205.

   to fish in reservoirs, 68.

   to sell milk, 164.

LICENSED OBSTRUCTIONS. See *Streets.*

LIGHTS. See *Lamps.*

LINCOLN BROOK, power over, 69.

LIVERY STABLES. See *Stables.*

LUMBER, inspection of may be regulated, 27.

   surveyor of, to be elected, 108.

LYNDE BROOK. See *Water.*

MACHINE SHOPS, erection of, 148.

MARSHAL. See *City Marshal.*

MAYOR, to be principal officer of the city, 3.

   with the aldermen and common council, to constitute the
      city council, 3.

   fiscal affairs, &c., vested in city council, 3.

   contracts with the city, 4 note 1.

   to be elected by the voters in ward meetings, 7.

   time of election, 8.

   votes for, to be counted, recorded, &c., in open ward-meet-
      ing, 8.

   term of office of, 7.

   30

STAGE COACH. See *Hackney Carriages*.
STANDS, for hay, straw, wood, bark, and charcoal, to be
    designated by mayor and aldermen, 196.
    sellers to stand only at the places designated, 196.
STATE OFFICERS, election of, 27.
STATUTES ADOPTED, 246.
STATUTES OF INCORPORATION. See *Acts of Incorpora-
    tion*.
STATUTES PUBLISHED. See *Acts Published*.
STEPS, not to obstruct streets, 208.
STONES, not to be thrown in streets, 210.
STRAW. See *Hay*.
STREETS.
  LAYING out, altering, and discontinuing.
    power of the city council in relation to, &c., 25.
    mayor and aldermen to act first, 25.
    width of streets, 26, 78, 201.
    manner of laying out, &c., 199, 200.
    to be laid out, only on petition, 199.
    notice to be given, 199.
    what notice shall specify, 199.
    all parties interested, to have a hearing, 200.
    proceedings before laying out, &c., 200.
    boundaries, to be fixed by mayor and aldermen, 200.
    damages, to be estimated before laying out, 200.
    stone monuments to be placed at angles, 201.
    damages, 25.
    under the betterment law, 25 note.
    laying out, in commons, &c., 25 note.
    appeals to, 25, 26 note 1.
  PRIVATE streets, to have grade fixed by city council, 201.
    city council may close the same, 201.
    abuttors to grade private streets, 77.
    proceedings in case of neglect or refusal, 77.
    grading, by the mayor and aldermen, not to be an accept-
    ance of the street, 78.
  STREETS, in general.
    commissioners of highways to have the care of, 113.

33

WORCESTER.—*Continued*.

duties of the town, &c., about schools, 24.

incorporated as a town, 1.

by-laws to remain in force, &c., 29.

WORCESTER GAS LIGHT COMPANY. See *Gas Light Company*.

WORCESTER PROTECTIVE DEPARTMENT, incorporated, 87.

powers and duties of, 87.

not to interfere with fire department, 88.

city council may regulate, 88.

www.ingramcontent.com/pod-product-compliance
Lightning Source LLC
Chambersburg PA
CBHW021104270326
41929CB00009B/729